THE VISIONBUILDERS' MANUAL

9 Steps to Panoramic Success for Your Company, Career, or Cause

Visionbuilders are saying...

"Your wisdom, and excellent guidance makes the Visionbuilders program valuable and life altering." - Ben Clark, senior management consultant

"Never have I had such clarity of the power of spawning and nurturing a vision." - Lloyd Weber, Financial Broker

"This short class provided enough specifics to be immediately useful." - Jenn Fay, yoga teacher

"Your delivery is fantastic! These steps can be used for anything, each one can be used on its own, and I can do them easily." - Bill Barbour, corporate board member

"If you are an entrepreneur or business owner seeking a larger vision for greater business opportunities ...The first speaker, Rev. Margaret Shepherd, was worth the entire price of admission." - Rob Yamaguchi, Yamaguchi Advertising

"Thank you for your inspiring, dynamic and informative presentation at EMERGE. Looking forward to reading your book." - Irena Cole, Pre-Paid Legal Services

"I took Margaret's day long workshop and I learned so much that I didn't want to leave! The Visionbuilder's teachings have helped my spirit immeasurably but also MEASURABLY, my pocketbook has grown as a result of her gracious tutelage." - Tracy Weisert actress/singer

THE VISIONBUILDERS' MANUAL

9 Steps to Panoramic Success for
Your Company, Career, or Cause

Margaret J. Shepherd

NEW YORK

THE VISIONBUILDERS' MANUAL
9 Steps to Panoramic Success for Your Company, Career, or Cause

Cover Design by: 3 Dog Design   www.3dogdesign.net
Author photos by: Deb Halberstadt, HalfCity Productions
www.halfcityproductions.com

ISBN 978-1-60037-750-1
Library of Congress Control Number: 2010920397

Morgan James Publishing
1225 Franklin Ave., STE 325
Garden City, NY 11530-1693
Toll Free 800-485-4943
www.MorganJamesPublishing.com

Dedication

This book is dedicated to you, visionbuilders who have dedicated yourselves to your visions, and to future visionbuilders who will succeed using this program. It is equally dedicated to my family, especially my husband, Earl J. Waits. I am my best because of you. It is my hope that this book honors the colleagues who constantly inspire and teach me in our field of personal and business success.

Contents

INTRODUCTION

The common idea that success spoils people by making them vain, egotistic and self-complacent is erroneous; on the contrary it makes them, for the most part, humble, tolerant and kind. It is failure that makes people bitter and cruel.

—W. Somerset Maugham

Let's agree. Success is good for us. It's good for our customers and employees and for our investors and suppliers. It's good for our personal relationships, health, and well-being. It's good for the world at large. Maugham is right. Success brings out the best in us.

It's the *path* to success that can bring out the worst in us—our deepest fears, our worst behavior, and our greatest pain. Can't the path be as fulfilling and as much fun as the prize?

Finding the answer to that question has been my passion for decades.

I am a student of success—organizations and individuals who achieve it effortlessly, those who suffer for it, and those who never find it. I've studied my clients' experiences and my own. What have I learned? I've found five truths that are the bottom line of success.

1. Success is natural; failure is learned.
2. Vision is the ultimate success catapult.
3. Mindset is the biggest success barrier.

4.   Self-mastery is the most important skill set.

5.   Whole-brain intelligence is the secret of champions

In this book you'll learn that an authentic vision stands above any other means to success. Vision is an almost magical transcendent power. The right vision dissolves inner and outer barriers and inspires the courage to change. Vision opens the door to struggle-free, pain-free success. You'll learn that, once that door is open, a success mindset, self-mastery, and the right skills complete the process of making vision real.

You'll learn a simple system for getting clear on the right vision for right now and getting the practical tools that bring it to life. You'll gain skills for disciplining your mind so that you stay strong. You'll harness principles that govern how beliefs and emotions create experiences. You'll learn to create visionary success for every aspect of your life. Most important, you'll discover that the answer to the question "Can't the path be as fulfilling and as much fun as the prize?" is a loud and happy YES!

You'll meet visionbuilders who have decided to change their minds about who they are, how life works, and what's possible. They've used that new way of thinking to create a new way of being—one that guarantees success.

Who are visionbuilders? They are leaders who want to better their company or their cause, career-changers who want to choose what's next and how to get there, teams who want to build a shared vision, and personal growth seekers who want a better experience of life. Anyone who is ready to fulfill the inborn instinct to create and contribute and have fun in the process can be a visionbuilder.

Mindset Makes or Breaks Your Vision

One of my favorite cartoons shows three card players around a table. Boys' night out? One is smoking, wearing a dingy T-shirt and a five o'clock shadow. Another, middle-aged, balding and paunchy, has more empty beer cans than poker chips in his spot. Both players are eyeing the third. We can see the hand he is holding. Four aces. We also see he has no beer or cigars but, instead, a water dish. He is a dog. Sitting upright on his chair, holding his cards tightly between his front paws, his floppy ears are flat to his head and his eyes are level. He does not smile or frown. Then we notice his tail. It is a blur of motion, wagging furiously, thumping against his chair. The caption reads, "Despite his skillful playing, Benny would never truly master the game until he could perfect the art of the poker tail."

The cartoon makes us chuckle because it's a twist on the legendary "poker face" that prevents players from displaying their feelings on their faces and giving away clues about the cards they hold. The poker face—or poker tail—is a valuable skill in poker games. But in the rest of life it's more or less useless because of an important principle that visionbuilders know. Even the most inscrutable poker face can't hide the contents of your mindset, because your life is on display. Every circumstance of your life is a display of your beliefs and attitudes. No exceptions.

Have you tried success-building programs before and gotten nothing but frustration for your efforts? Most of us have. You didn't fail because you didn't work hard enough, or you weren't smart enough, or the program was bad. Even the best tools and strategies fail without the right mindset. In later chapters, you'll read about studies showing that positive affirmations actually made some subjects feel worse instead of better. Mindset is why. Your mindset, the set of beliefs and attitudes that filter how you perceive the world, affects how you do everything. If you don't have a success mindset, failure is guaranteed. The right mindset is crucial to success.

Why is it so important? Without a success mindset, you risk sabotaging your vision. A mindset containing beliefs that support failure can't support success. No matter how much you try, you'll sabotage your efforts. Your mindset is always in charge.

The Visionbuilders' Program

The visionbuilders' program teaches you how to succeed by building a vision. "An imagined ideal you want more than you fear change," a vision uplifts, inspires, and focuses, making it easier to overcome inner and outer barriers to success. But a few things have to go right. Thoughts have to support success and not failure. You need all hands on deck mentally—both logic and intuition. You have to aim at the right vision and make sure you have the right mindset so that your actions match your intentions. The program helps individuals and organizations get these right.

The visionbuilders' program doesn't just teach—it transforms. Starting with establishing the right mindset, nine skills identify your vision and bring it to life in a systematic, measurable, repeatable way. You'll learn how to align with universal principles and create positive self-fulfilling prophesies. You'll learn to use whole-brain intelligence, engaging both intuition and logic for better decisions. The visionbuilders' program is a system for creating vision after vision, in business and in every area of life.

Often success programs require that you become more self-aware: "I am this way or that way" or "This is a belief pattern I need to change." They focus on understanding why you are the way you are: "This in my history caused me to believe X instead of Y." It is the same for organizational development programs—there is a heavy focus on analyzing the "whys" in hopes that the answers lead to "what to do" to improve things.

The visionbuilders' program increases awareness, but with a difference. You become more aware of *what*, not necessarily *why*. The process is to describe current reality objectively and then choose a preferred reality. Instead of *why* questions, you ask, "What's happening now?" and "What would I/we prefer?" No deep analysis required and no criticism allowed. Visionbuilding isn't about meeting an external standard or fixing problems, but about living a vision.

This book is organized into three sections that follow the visionbuilders' process.

    I. The Foundation. Four chapters work together to establish a success mindset. That mindset creates a "happy brain" that makes change easy. You'll learn that you were born hardwired for success and you'll find out how to recapture that innate power. We are all subject to universal creative principles. You'll learn how they can work in your favor, including the invisible laws of money.

    II. The Model. This is the "how-to" blueprint. The visionbuilders' success triangle details the three keys to visionbuilding and how they combine to guarantee success. The center is the vision and the sides are self mastery, mindset, and whole-brain skills.

    III. Visionbuilders' Skills. This is a set of nine unique skills that build vision, first in imagination and then in reality. The skills manage your thoughts and emotions so that your success mindset stays strong. They put in place structures and systems that support your vision. They make sure actions match intentions and measure results along the way. Additional chapters teach how to build business vision, and they provide bonus tools, with special skills for blind spots, sharp turns, and quicksand along the way. There's a chapter containing self-tests for understanding your current realities.

Premises and Promises

How you feel about the underlying philosophy of something you're considering matters, whether it's a success program, a business, an organization, a religion, or a mate. Your feelings can affect your commitment and ultimately your success. By understanding the philosophical foundation of the visionbuilders' program, you can decide how you feel about it and proceed from there. Of course, I hope you'll wholeheartedly agree with what you see. But all that's really necessary is a willingness to work with the program, because your commitment will grow with your positive results. There's magic in an open mind.

I call the foundation principles "Premises and Promises." They are the premises on which the program is built, and they are promises because the more you accept, believe, understand, integrate, and metabolize them, the more success you can promise yourself.

If you find some of these hard to accept, perhaps you've been taught something different and don't want to change. I'm certain that if you approach the principles with an open mind and open heart, you will find that new ways of thinking can catapult you to a better life. There are explanations and illustrations throughout this book, so don't worry if the principles bring up questions. Trust that you'll find answers as you go along.

Look at the principles and ask yourself "How might it help me to believe this?" and "Can it hurt me to believe this?" Let your honest response guide you. Then you'll feel safe to explore them.

Visionbuilders' Foundation Principles

1. You are more than your finite human experience. You are an individualized part of the universe, inseparable from all life.
2. It is your nature to create and contribute. Success is your birthright and destiny.
3. You are hardwired for success. Success is natural; failure is learned.
4. Impersonal universal laws respond to your thoughts and emotions to create your experiences. You take charge of your life by taking charge of your mindset.
5. Emotions are the power behind thoughts. You change your emotions (and brain chemistry) by changing your thoughts.

6. Every experience in your life is one that you created, invited, attracted, accepted, promoted, permitted, expanded, or allowed. No exceptions.

7. Genuine intuition reveals flawless insight, clarity, and guidance. You are always connected to the universe through intuition. Intuition, plus reasoned logic, form whole-brain intelligence—that is your greatest power.

8. The right mindset, skills, and personal mastery are the requirements for success. Struggle and suffering are not.

9. Your authentic desires and vision come fully resourced. You need only say yes.

10. What serves one, serves all. What is authentically right and good for one person is equally right and good for all.

Definitions

Have you ever had to wonder what an author meant by certain terms? I have, and it made the book less valuable to me. I didn't like guessing at what wasn't clearly defined. What if I guessed wrong? It was distracting and frustrating. I want to be sure you don't have that experience. The following are definitions of terms in *The Visionbuilders' Manual* that I want to clarify—so you don't have to guess.

Success: The complete fulfillment of your highest vision for any topic in life. That means any topic in any area of life: physical, emotional, mental, financial, spiritual, relationships, and work.

Vision: An ideal experience that you create in your mind, one that you want to make real, an experience that you want more than you fear change. It's like a scene from a movie that you want to live in. You can have a vision for anything that is important to you, grand or mundane, and more than one at a time. Dictionaries say vision is something seen with special perception, a revelation, prophesy, mental picture. The visionbuilders' process uses that special perception to reveal that vision that is real, never coming from fears or ego or "should's," or as a problem solution.

Visionbuilder: Dictionaries define "builder" as an architect, creator, initiator, inventor, leader, organizer, originator, prime mover, promoter, craftsman, artisan, designer, originator, planner, and strategist. You may not believe it yet, but, as a visionbuilder, you are all of these, or you become them along the way.

Universe: The eternal, all-knowing, all-seeing creative energy of love. To me, that means God, but I use a secular term in the visionbuilders' program for a reason. Even within religions, each person's understanding of God is individual and unique. And, for both believers and non-believers, the word itself can be emotionally charged. I don't want anything to get in the way of your access to the principles and tools in this book. Please substitute the word *God* for *the Universe* if that works for you, or, if you prefer a different word, use it instead.

Mindset: The contents of your consciousness, including your conscious and subconscious beliefs about yourself, how the world works, and the unseen universe. You can learn a lot about your mindset by looking at your life and asking yourself "To what degree am I creating my biggest dreams, experiences that make me fulfilled and happy and that give something good to the world?"

Success Mindset: The set of beliefs, attitudes and perceptions that will create any kind of success, including a vision.

Panoramic Success: A panorama is an unobstructed, complete view in every direction. Panoramic success means success that is unobstructed and complete, success that encompasses every area of life, all at once.

Wholeness: A state of mind. It means that your head and heart, your body, mind, desires, talents, even your fears and your "dark side" are integrated into your awareness. You have mental clarity, reliable intuition, emotional mastery, focus, good physical health, overall well-being, and a sunny view of life. The opposite of whole is fragmented. When you are fragmented, you don't make decisions easily or well, because you're not connected to your own wisdom; you're angry and don't know why, because you're not connected to your emotions; your body becomes ill, because you're not connected to its needs. Wholeness is harmony. Visionbuilding creates wholeness.

Universal Laws: Principles that are true for all of life—at least until new discoveries reveal otherwise. Scientists once convinced us it was "true" that the earth was flat; then new science proved a different truth. Universal laws include the laws of physics, thermodynamics, biology, systems dynamics, and the sciences of human behavior. The visionbuilders' program has scientific principles as its foundation. Chapter 4 shows you the science behind the laws of visionbuilding.

The Final Key

Imagine your visionbuilding journey. You're excited to think of your personal or business dreams becoming real. You learn the foundation principles, decide on your first vision to create, and start to practice the skills. The vision begins to take form and gains momentum. Soon you're experiencing success that feeds both your bank account and your soul. Working with others on a shared vision, you create success for your business, your team, or your cause. Both the result and the process make you happy. You realize that success doesn't require heroics, just a system for reconnecting to your natural genius for visionbuilding. This is the journey of a successful visionbuilder. I know it will be your journey, but I also know you will encounter fears masquerading as potholes and quicksand on the trail. Those are times of temptation. You may get frustrated and want to give up.

Maybe visionbuilders should be issued one of the new and controversial high-tech swimsuits, aptly called speedsuits. The 20 minutes it takes to wriggle into the thing pays off big. At the 2008 Olympics, 47 of the 51 world records went to wearers of these suits. What might one do for you? Would you zoom to success in record time? The controversy is whether the speedsuits create an unfair advantage, as if the fabric secretly delivers steroids directly into your muscles or extra intelligence to your brain.

I developed the visionbuilders' program to give you an advantage—a fair one—in fulfilling your most heartfelt visions. The principles and skills rack up wins for visionbuilders. Even so, sometimes you learn principles and skills but stay stuck. Why? Didn't the program give everyone an equal advantage? Olympian swimmer Markus Rogan of Austria has a great answer. Questioned about the fairness of the advantage the speedsuits provide, he said, "I tested it. I threw it in the pool and it didn't move at all. So I'll still have to swim." Right. Thank you, Markus. We can count up and count on all our advantages, but even with the best swimsuits or credentials or skills or connections, even with the visionbuilders' program, you've still got to get into the pool and swim.

Part I

Foundation

Chapter 1

HARDWIRED FOR SUCCESS!

Were you in Failure School with me—invisible classrooms where we learned lessons that kept us from our dreams? We attended unaware, as our culture planted messages in our subconscious minds—messages that would rule our lives.

Messages such as "Money is the root of all evil," "Always have a trade to fall back on," and "You have to suffer and struggle in order to succeed" diminished your power. They sent your imagination into hiding and suppressed your uniqueness. You learned to struggle and suffer, chasing someone else's definition of success. You learned an "either-or" rule about fulfillment and money: "You can have the fulfilling job at poor pay, or the job with big bucks that doesn't feed your soul. One or the other, but not both." There was the "can't have it all" rule about success in the full panorama of life: "You can succeed in one or two areas, but never in every area of life all at once." You learned to expect that if you have good health and prosperity, you won't have happy relationships and a fulfilling work life or spiritual peace at the same time. So when you lose your job, your spouse runs off with your best friend, and your oldest kid goes to jail, you tell yourself, "Oh well, at least I have my health," because subconsciously you believe you can't have it all. There were conflicting messages as well, such as "Be a good person" versus "Nice guys/gals finish last"!

Are these familiar? You learned them all during a lifetime of Failure School. Everybody did. They are embedded in our collective culture and in your own subconscious mind, sometimes with no effect, but most often causing trouble. Failure School messages continue to be reinforced and retaught as you go about your life unaware.

The more you absorb the lessons of Failure School, the more self-sabotage keeps your life small and safe. Do you have to stay enrolled? No! You don't have to live your life from those old lessons for one more minute! You can flunk out of Failure School for good. This book teaches you how.

My name for those who fail at Failure School is Success Heroes. They aren't all mega-rich, superfamous, or saviors of humankind; some live humbly and simply. But they all share the experience of panoramic success. They're financially free, healthy in mind–body–spirit, with fulfilling work and caring relationships. They don't believe in "either-or" or "can't have it all" or any other life-diminishing lessons. They are happy and at peace; they have the inner and outer riches we all want and deserve. By this definition, who are your personal Success Heroes? When you look at your own life, to what degree are you one? Until now, how well have you *failed* at Failure School?

How do Success Heroes achieve their dreams without struggle or suffering? Luckily for us, they leave clues. I've studied Success Heroes for years and found consistent commonalities. There are three attributes common to Success Heroes:

1.   A vision
2.   Success mindset
3.   Self-mastery

A heartfelt, authentic vision drives Success Heroes. They are inspired by a desire to create an ideal experience that they see in their mind's eye. They believe in their own power to create their dreams, because they have a success mindset—a set of beliefs that overpower Failure School lessons. As they pursue their vision, they master their emotions and trust their inner guidance, even when it goes against so-called facts and even when they're afraid.

Success Heroes have skills and tools you might not have learned yet, and you'll have your own Failure School lessons to overcome. The visionbuilders' program is designed to help you unlearn Failure School lessons while you learn skills for success.

How can an average person, who absorbed Failure School lessons about how life works and what's possible, become a Success Hero? How can an authentic vision, a success mindset, and self-mastery create panoramic success?

Success is natural; it's failure that is learned. You and I can become Success Heroes because success is our natural state, and we can return to that natural state at any time. We are born with a relentless natural impetus for success. It is always at work, inspiring you to reach for your highest potential and express your greatness. You are always attracting resources that move your dreams forward. You are hardwired for success.

Dictionaries describe hardwiring as logic circuitry that is permanently fixed by the wiring of the hardware, as opposed to being programmable in software or controlled by a switch. What is hardwired can't be modified or changed once it's installed. Your innate success destiny is like that: it's hardwired into your being. The lessons of Failure School or any other negative messages or life experiences can't change that hardwiring.

.

SUCCESS is natural.

FAILURE is learned.

Oprah Winfrey overcame a childhood of poverty and abuse to become one of the most powerful communicators on the planet. Mathematician John Nash won a Nobel Prize, although mental demons tormented him most of his life. The brilliance of scientist Stephen Hawking was not dimmed by his diseased and deteriorating body.

How were these famous Success Heroes able to achieve so much against such odds? They returned to their original hardwiring. They let go of belief in lack or limitation and stood in the truth of their own innate power. They believed in themselves and in their vision of what they wanted to create. They claimed the success that was their natural destiny.

You were born to create and contribute, and you are hardwired for success. If you are not experiencing joyful success, fulfillment, prosperity, and peace of mind in every area of life, you are blocking your natural destiny.

Maybe you have tried many methods and systems and tools, but you are still repeating the same painful patterns. Maybe you think you can't have the life you want, no matter what you do or how hard you try. You blame yourself or others, or you blame your circumstances. Still, somehow you know you are capable of creating something better and that you have more within you than you are using. There is a powerful genius within you, waiting to ignite your life. Vision is the fuel. Vision burns through the fears and doubts that block your destiny of success.

Good Reasons for Bad Times on the Road to Success

There are lots of good reasons why we struggle and suffer on the way to success and many good reasons why some of us go to our graves unfulfilled. But math isn't destiny. Adding up these reasons doesn't make you their permanent victim. With the right vision, mindset, and tools, anyone can create success in every area of life. Anyone can become a Success Hero.

Among the good reasons we get stuck are:

1. **No vision.**

    When Helen Keller was asked if there was anything worse than being blind, she replied, "Yes: having no vision." If you aren't clear on your true desires for any area of life, you are living life blind. You live your default life—the life your current beliefs create. It's not always easy to know what you really want. But it is easy to drift along with the mainstream and just let life happen.

2. **Looking for success in all the wrong places.**

    One of our Failure School lessons is that success comes only with the right conditions met – the right education, the right connections, and hard work. Yet, I'll bet you can list a dozen people who have perfect credentials and connections and who work like mad but still aren't successful. Maybe you even include yourself on that list. We are taught to believe that working hard to create the right outer circumstances rewards us with success. No! It's your inner circumstances that matter. And that's what has to change if you want more success in life. My students named this "Margaret's Most Maddening Truth," and you'll see it throughout in this book: Every experience in your life is one that you created, invited, attracted accepted, promoted, expanded, or allowed. No exceptions.

3.   **Believing the myth of vending-machine metaphysics.**

You know the myth: Insert a positive affirmation, and your heart's desire plops into the dispenser tray. Nowadays, most of us know about the Law of Attraction, but although it's a simple principle, it's not always easy to harness. Lots of variables can affect your outcomes. Several studies about those variables are discussed in later chapters. It's true that your thoughts are creative, but your attitudes and emotions behind those thoughts determine your results. That's why the right mindset is part of the visionbuilders' motto for success: "Aim right, think right, act right."

4.   **You're stuck in your comfort zone.**

Oh, how we love our comfort zones—our preferred way of looking at the world and our beliefs about what's so. They keep us feeling safe and at peace. Most of us have lived there so long we can't imagine what's outside it. Even if we can, it scares us silly, so we stay safe and stuck. No matter how unhappy and unfulfilled we may be, anything is better than the unknown territory of change. Of course, there's a catch: Everything you want lies just outside your comfort zone.

And the big one . . .

5. **You went to Failure School.**

> We all did—we unwittingly learned those lessons of how to fail instead of how to succeed. Failure School, as described, is what you must overcome in order to create the panoramic success that is your birthright. Unless you do, no success program will work, because Failure School subconscious dogma will sabotage it.

These five good reasons are a recipe for struggle, suffering, and failure. You need a better recipe—the recipe for reclaiming your birthright success. That recipe is the right vision, the right mindset, the right whole-brain skills, and the self-mastery to use them.

The visionbuilders' program works where other programs fall short, because it is that recipe. Its motto is "Aim right. Think right. Act right." Aim right—aim your attention at the right vision. Think right—use the right mental skills that control fears and ego. Act right—take the right actions to make your vision real.

Whatever area of life you chose for your first visionbuilding experience, the program walks you through a systematic, step-by-step process just as you'd build a building. First is the concept of the building—that's your vision. Then come the architectural and construction principles—that's the visionbuilders' foundation principles. Then the blueprint and construction plans follow—that's the Success Triangle. Finally, construction materials, tools, and a skilled labor force–that's you with the visionbuilders' skill set. Once these elements are in place, you can use them to build any vision for your personal life, your business, or organization. You know how to aim right, think right, and act right, so you guarantee yourself panoramic success.

If you've gone shopping anytime after 1907, you've probably been in a store called JC Penny's or its predecessor, The Golden Rule Stores (don't you love that name?). James Cash Penny was born in 1875 to a poor farming family in Missouri, the seventh of twelve children. When he turned eight, his father told him it was time to buy his own clothes. Perhaps at an age when his success hardwiring was yet uncorrupted, the boy promptly bought a pig, fattened it up, sold it at a profit, and bought school clothes. With the remaining funds he purchased several more pigs, fattened them, sold them, and bought more. Soon he had a successful and expanding business. But the young entrepreneur got a lesson in business ups and downs when neighbors complained about the . . . um . . . aroma of his inventory. Out of the pig business but still on a roll, he farmed and sold watermelons.

After high school graduation he landed a sales job in a local dry goods store, happy for the opportunity to learn more about business. Never physically robust, at age 20 Penny moved west to strengthen his health. He found employment in Colorado, in dry goods again. Soon he had saved enough to fulfill his dream of owning his own business. He opened a butcher shop. But a hard lesson was waiting. He knew the importance of sticking to your values but learned that righteousness doesn't guarantee success. Penny refused to pay bribes of whiskey to a local hotel in exchange for its business. Apparently it was a powerful hotel, because Penny was soon bankrupt, jobless, and broke.

His inborn success hardwiring, his values, and his dreams moved him forward. He found work with a local mercantile company and became a valuable employee. Soon he was given a store to run and then a one-third partnership in that store. Penny didn't give up on his vision, and, before long, he was able to buy the Golden Rule Stores Company. In 1913 he renamed it the JC Penny Company and went on to legendary success. In 1924 the 500th store opened, and, by 1971, 1,660 stores bore the JC Penny sign.

Between those years and store openings was the 1929 stock market crash. Penney lost $40 million when banks foreclosed on his loans. Selling off what he could, he faced a $7 million debt at the age of 56. He borrowed money and started over, and soon the JC Penny Company rose again.

Penny died in 1971 at the age of 95. His enormous legacy includes a lesson for visionbuilders. A compelling vision, self-mastery, and a success mindset keep our innate success hardwiring going strong.

Flowing with your vision is magical. It's like swimming downstream with the natural current of your inborn knack for success. I invite you to find a vision that excites you and then to take your seat in it. Strap yourself in for the ride of your life. Soon you'll be building vision after vision. Life will be a constant flow of creating and contributing what brings you joy. You will realize that you have become your own Success Hero. And you will smile.

Chapter 2

BUILDING VISION

When you are inspired by some great purpose, some extraordinary project, all your thoughts break their bonds. Your mind transcends limitations, your consciousness expands in every direction, and you find yourself in a new, great and wonderful world. Dormant forces, faculties and talents become alive and you discover yourself to be a greater person by far than you ever dreamed yourself to be.

—Patanjali (Indian poet, third century BCE)

Vision is the ultimate success catapult! Vision uplifts, inspires, and focuses. It is an alchemy more powerful than goals or dreams. The most daunting inner and outer success barriers die a fast death in vision's heat. Vision can heal psychological wounds, physical maladies, and broken relationships. Vision injects purpose and passion into failing lives and businesses. It is vision that we can thank for innovation and creativity in all fields.

Dictionaries say vision is something seen with special perception. It is a revelation, a prophesy, a mental picture of what can be— possibilities beyond the status quo. Vision is considered a trait of exceptional leaders and entrepreneurs.

During years of working with individuals and corporations, bringing visions to life, I've come to define a vision as a unique, imagined, ideal experience for any human topic, a blueprint that draws resources to itself and sets in motion the transcendent power of joy.

In a practical sense, a vision is an imagined, ideal experience that you want more than you fear change. Vision compels change, yet change is something we commonly resist. I have a theory that change triggers subconscious fears of annihilation; that's why we resist it so fiercely. Regardless of the reason, vision sets two opposing forces in motion: desire for the vision, with its change requirements, and the visionbuilder's resistance to change.

For the vision to win, a few things have to go right. Only the right vision can thrill you right through your fears. Only the right mindset prevents self- sabotage. Only whole-brain intelligence and high levels of self-mastery engage the skills that build a vision.

Inauthentic Vision

There's a difference between a vision inspired by compelling ideals and one conjured from fears, vague wishes, "should's," or problems that you need to solve. Then there's the question of where to find a vision. It's common to think of deciding on a vision as a mental, mechanical process. Visions generated in that fashion have limited potential. If you've ever suffered through a corporate meeting where you were expected to "buy into" a vision that had no real meaning for you, you know what I mean. The wrong vision fails to inspire. Instead, commitment comes through obligation, fear, or guilt. Even if you're committed, it's easy to head off in the wrong direction and fall into the first pothole. There's just no magic in the wrong vision.

When you hike in the woods, it's smart to know what poison ivy and poisonous snakes look like. An inauthentic vision can give you at least as much trouble, so you'd better be able to recognize one. Recognizing the signposts with key aspects of an inauthentic vision will let you start your vision quest in relative safety. Chapter 9 provides more help, with a detailed list of vision authenticity questions.

The following are signposts of an inauthentic vision:

- It is a "should"—something you believe you *should* want, according to some standard or external imperative.
- It is a reaction to what you don't want. You decide on something you want in the future because of something you don't like in the present.
- It is the means instead of the ultimate result—confusion between the vision itself and the steps or resources you think you need to achieve it.
- It comes from competition—wanting to achieve or acquire something because of what somebody else does or has.

Authentic Vision

Vision is not analytic, it is intuitive. It is knowing, in your bones, what can or must be done. Vision isn't forecasting the future; it is creating the future by taking action in the present.

—James Collins and Jerry Porras:
Built to Last: Successful Habits of Visionary Companies.

The key is to start with a vision that is heartfelt and authentic. Authentic vision comes from within—from the inner essence of an individual or organization. It is intrinsic, not relative to an outer something or someone. It is not a goal you think up, as in a "brainstorm," but more of a "spiritstorm," revealing the inner spirit of its author and perceived through a whole-brain, big-picture kind of intelligence. That goes for corporate, political, financial, and organizational visions as well as personal ones. The same inner wisdom inspires and advances them all.

Authentic vision is richly complex. It has material effects, emotional depth, intellectual stimulation, service aspects, and even a spiritual essence. One of the vision authenticity questions you'll find in Chapter 9 is whether the vision blesses beyond one's life.

A sense of purpose is another aspect of authentic vision. You will feel like the vision is the immediate purpose of your life. It pulls you in and compels you forward toward its fulfillment. I like Peter Senge's distinction between vision and purpose: "Purpose is abstract. Vision is concrete" (Peter Senge, *The Fifth Discipline*). For example, your purpose might be "I support higher education for the poor," but your *vision* might be "My foundation generates enough money to fund ten scholarships a year."

Authentic vision expresses uniqueness. Each individual is a unique combination of talents and possibilities, and every business has a unique founding dream. The right vision nudges that uniqueness into greater expression. There is symbiosis between inherent uniqueness and vision, each nourishing the other. Your unique combination of math and verbal talents leads you to a particular career that further develops those talents. The unique founding ideas of a business lead it to a particular path of growth that strengthens and expands those ideas—think Apple Computer or Amazon, or the unstoppable trajectory of James Cash Penny. It is our defining uniqueness that helps us know that "Yes, this is the right vision for right now."

The Alchemy of Vision

Whether by alchemy, magic, chemistry, or grace, an authentic vision will transcend or transform anything obstructing its fulfillment. The joy of an authentic vision is its power.

A vision operates like the flexible fierceness of water. If water needs to be a torrential falls, sweeping away what would stop its flow, it is that. If it needs to be a gentle pressure, shaping streamed rocks over eons of time, it is that. If it needs to go around, under, or above an obstacle because that's the smartest path, it does.

As a visionbuilder, you will let your vision lead you and transform you because you want its fulfillment more than you fear change.

Seeking a vision will always mean you want two things that are in opposition to each other, causing tension. Psychologists call this "cognitive dissonance," a conflict between divergent desires that must find resolution. You want to build muscles by going to the gym, but you also want to stay home and watch TV. What happens next? Your mind goes to work to resolve the conflict until one side wins. You say you're too tired to go to the gym, and, besides, bulky muscles look ugly. Staying home wins. Or, you say muscles will make me feel healthier and happier than a nap. The gym wins.

Vision always creates a state of tension between itself and perceived current reality—change versus no change. It creates a gap between what you want and what you currently have. This is what that tension looks like:

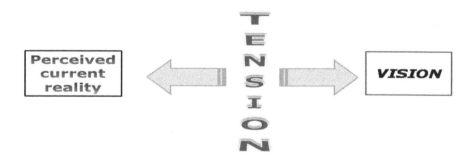

That gap is tension that you can break in two ways. Let go of one side or the other. (If you let go of both, the energy is gone, and you can't proceed.) You break the tension by choosing. Go to the gym or stay home.

Tension is energy. It's how you perceive that energy that gets visionbuilders in trouble. Energy itself is neutral. You can use it any way you want. Tension energy can equal many different experiences: anxiety, stress, worry, excitement, fun, and creativity. Perhaps because of our natural change resistance, most of us perceive tension in the worst way, making our visionbuilding challenge worse than it has to be.

When a vision is authentic, magic can happen. Remember our definition of a vision, "an imagined, ideal experience that you want more than you fear change." Because the nature of vision is joy, your vision makes you happy when you think about it. Those good feelings create what I describe in Chapter 6 as a "happy brain." A surge of powerful brain chemicals creates a positive addiction to the thought that has made you feel joy. If your brain is happy enough, it can overpower or transcend the fears that are vying for control.

The more authentic the vision is, the happier the thoughts will be. The happier the thoughts are, the stronger the positive addiction is. The stronger the positive addiction is, the more it overpowers fear of change. Voilà—the vision happens!

Building Vision

Follow your bliss and the Universe will open doors where there were only walls.

—Joseph Campbell

Successful visionbuilders possess an authentic vision, a success mindset, whole-brain skills, and self-mastery. Visionbuilders "work easy," not hard, because they know success is their natural state and fun—if you let it be.

Vision is created like all life experiences, through mental energy. Life exists in the invisible realm first and then takes form in human experience. Once you become familiar with the principles that rule the process, you'll realize that you've known them all your life. Visionbuilders relearn how to use them consciously to create the life experiences they want most. Chapter 3 shows you how.

Visionbuilding Is "Inspansion"

There was a sales manager who wanted to expand one of his territories. The former sales representative had just retired. He had always insisted the territory would never be worth more than $200,000 in annual revenues. No matter how much the manager encouraged him, trained him, and supported him, the territory never produced more than $200,000 a year. Interviewing for a new rep, the manager asked candidates what they thought the territory could be worth. One named a figure over $300,000. "That's my guy," thought the manager. One year later, that newly hired rep had expanded the territory's revenues to $350,000. How did that happen? Unlike the former rep, he had an inner picture of business expanding and a belief that it was possible. That mental "inspansion" created the revenue expansion.

Your life will be as big or small as your biggest and smallest thoughts. I made up the word *inspansion* to describe the inner expansion process of building a vision in your mind. Expansion is external growth, reaching outward to create your dreams. Expansion can't happen, however, unless your inner thoughts expand first. The quality of your "inspansion" determines the quality of your expansion.

When you have an idea about an experience, it forms a template in your mind. Sometimes it's called a mental equivalent. Mental equivalents are part of your mindset, the inner beliefs that create your experiences. I like the term "mental equivalent" because it's so descriptive. Your mind creates the template of your beliefs, and the equivalent of that template takes form as your experience. Chapter 3 explains the principles behind it as the Law of Mindset Mirroring.

You lose excess weight then regain it because you lack the right mental equivalent to sustain the new reality you want. The mental template of you at a certain weight keeps operating until you change it. Lottery winners lose their fortunes because they haven't created the new mental equivalent that will sustain their new wealth. Like the former sales rep, people try to succeed in business and fail because they haven't created the necessary mental equivalents for success. "Inspansion" creates the right mental equivalents. Without it, you continue to create from your present mental equivalents.

Inspansion happens when you consciously expand your thoughts, ignore fears and doubts, think bigger, and imagine your vision clearly in your mind. It sometimes means believing in impossible possibilities. As Lewis Carroll wrote in *Through the Looking Glass* (1872), "Sometimes I've believed as many as six impossible things before breakfast."

Visionbuilding Is Transcending Fears

> *Fear is lack of faith. Lack of faith is ignorance. Fear can only be cured by vision.*
> —Horace Traubel: *Elbert Hubbard's Scrapbook,* 1923

The alchemy of vision is about the power of joy to overcome inner fears and outer obstacles. Let's take a closer look at fears so that, as the saying goes, we can "know thine enemy." We all have hidden fears that get activated with our desires to be, do, or have something new. Failed visionbuilding means that hidden fears have gotten the upper hand and sabotaged the plan. Visionbuilders learn to move their fears to the back of the bus and put their vision in the driver's seat.

Fears are not all the same—and not all are bad for you or your vision. Healthy fears keep you from snorkeling near hungry sharks and hitchhiking in bad neighborhoods. Ego-based fears keep you from asking for help, raising your prices, getting out on that dance floor, falling in love, or changing your ways. Healthy fears preserve your life. Ego-based fears preserve your self-importance. Both ego-based or irrational life preservation fears can gain a foothold in your subconscious and prevent you from living your vision.

Fears can cause you to doubt or criticize your vision. In *Setting Your Genius Free,* author Dick Richards says that your genius is not what you might wish it to be, it is simply what it is. When you begin to judge it, that binds you to what others might think of it, and then you are lost. His words apply to vision, too, which, in a sense, is an expression of your genius or your organization's genius. The voice of fear whispers, "What if my vision isn't grand enough, or significant enough, or holy enough. What if it doesn't have any sizzle? What if it's just puny? I'll be so embarrassed!" You can see the folly of anything less than unconditional love for your vision.

Visionbuilders learn to play tricks on their fears. As previously described, an exciting vision creates a happy brain, which will transcend fears almost magically. Still, you have to keep that magical vision front and center in your mind or else fears will sneak back in. The visionbuilders' skill set keeps you in control.

Visionbuilding Expresses Feelings Vs. Emotions

A distinction between emotions and feelings may seem trivial, but it's an important aspect of vision that helps develop self mastery.

It's your emotions, not your thoughts, words, or deeds that have the most power to create your circumstances. Emotions are your strongest energy, and the nature of your energy becomes the nature of your experiences. Even the best intentions—if they are offered with anger—create angry circumstances. Emotions rule.

Faced with a new long drive to work every day, my client affirmed, "I am happy commuting to my new job." Inwardly, though, she was miserable. The negative feeling overpowered her positive affirmation, and she continued to suffer on her commute. Did she ever resolve her suffering? Yes, but only when she learned to turn her emotions around. The visionbuilders' skills teach you how.

The new business coach, trying to launch her business, visualized clients until she got a headache, but her fearful energy about being a coach kept her stuck. The fear negated the visualization's power. Was she ever able to attract clients? Yes, but only when she took charge of her emotional state were those visualizations able to take form in reality.

Emotions come from the ego and are rooted in fears. A list of emotions includes anger, jealousy, frustration, shyness, hostility, surface happiness, surface satisfaction, despair, infatuation, and "cheap thrills." On the other hand, feelings come from the heart and are rooted in love. A list of feelings includes compassion, generosity, inclusiveness, fulfillment, peacefulness, acceptance, unconditional love, sadness, and joy.

Because authentic vision comes from the spiritual essence of yourself or your organization, you can see how its nature would be to express authentic feelings. If you examine the values and philosophies of respected successful organizations, you'll recognize the list that defines feelings.

Emotional mastery is a big part of the overall self-mastery that is a component of the visionbuilders' program. By preventing or controlling emotions that stall success, authentic feelings are free to emerge. Those genuine feelings make visionbuilding easier, because they match the essence of every vision.

Visionbuilding Is Managing What Stimulates Your Mind

Visionbuilding is as much about avoiding what derails your vision as it is about pursuing what promotes it. The human mind needs stimulation; it is a natural and healthy craving. We are always on the lookout for excitement; it's how we define excitement that marks our differences.

We get into trouble by not taking charge of the kind of stimulation that we allow to penetrate our heads. If you are not exposing yourself to what nourishes your vision, your mind will find whatever stimulation it can. It's not very discriminating in that regard; it's promiscuous and easily seduced. It is easier and faster to find stimulation in drama, crises, insults, illness, or injuries—your own or those of others.

Even with its transformative powers, it takes effort to build a vision. If you want your ideal to take form, you have to be as loyal and committed to it as you would to your most important relationships. You have to protect it from threats, including threats from yourself. That means if you are building a vision of a new career, you don't allow yourself to be stimulated by dramas in your current career. Wrest your attention away and plant it firmly in the vision you want to create, letting that be your stimulation instead. If you have a vision of a healthier body, don't be stimulated by your maladies, but move your mind to the positive stimulation of the vitality you seek.

You have choices about what you allow to stimulate your mind. Will you study marketing principles or watch cops-and-robbers TV? Will you discuss the next step in your self- improvement plan or will you gossip? You always have a choice. Visionbuilders learn to ask the power question many times a day: "Does this serve my vision?"

Visionbuilding Transcends Surface Personality

Whether you are an individual or a business, when your vision is more important than your surface personality, you will succeed. Yes, you read that right. A surface personality, in people and organizations, is a way of being, on the surface, to maintain a desired image. Beneath the surface are ideals, desires, and qualities that are the defining uniqueness of the person or the business. But they're invisible because of the veneer of the constructed image shown to the world.

A good way to look at the process of change is that it is only your surface personality that you are changing. The real you is under that surface, the you that is your defining uniqueness. When you want your vision more than you want to hold onto your surface personality, you will be able to allow the real you to shine forth, and, as a result, change will be easy.

Visionbuilding Is Inner Work First, Outer Work Second

When love and skill work together expect a masterpiece.
—John Ruskin: *Elbert Hubbard's Scrap Book*, 1923

The nine visionbuilders' skills include both inner and outer skills, or contemplation skills and action skills. Successful visionbuilding requires acute focus on your vision. Because a vision is revealed and crafted first in your mind and because self-mastery and mindset management are mental efforts, that is where the work begins—and where it returns when U-turns are necessary.

That might seem obvious, but most of us operate in reverse order. We spend only minimum time deciding what we want to accomplish, then roar out the door and have at it. The world responds. Oops—not the response we wanted. We react and try a new action. The world responds again—another reaction and another new action. When we've been battered around enough to wake us up, we pause to think, and maybe realize that "Think first, act second" would have been a better plan. I don't mean to imply that using gut instincts in the moment isn't effective—it is, but it's especially effective when that moment is one of stillness and calm.

When we start with inner processes that reveal an authentic vision and then expand and anchor it in our mind, we do ourselves a big favor. Outer actions that come from inner contemplation are destined for success, and we are destined for an easier and more enjoyable time of it. The ideal is to take actions only if you believe that they will support your vision, pay attention to the feedback, and measure it against your vision. Then adjust your actions according to inner guidance (whole-brain intelligence) and act again: inner work first, outer action second. You can even find this principle on bumper stickers and T-shirts: "Engage brain before firing mouth" and "Ready. Fire. Aim. Oops!"

The Experience of Visionbuilding

Whether you are an entrepreneur wanting to accelerate your business without burnout, a personal growth seeker, a not-for-profit organization leader, or a career changer, the following are some of the experiences that visionbuilders share:

- You don't build a vision—it builds you. Visionbuilding inspires personal evolution—you become less influenced by others and more influenced by inner wisdom. You stay flexible and fluid, yet anchored by vision. As you focus less on your surface personality and more on your vision, a deeper maturity emerges. Visionbuilders are open, trusting, humble, compassionate, brave, and healthy in mind-body-spirit. They are happy!
- Visionbuilding transcends politics. Personal influence and manipulation lose their relevance, because the vision becomes the authority. The vision becomes the personal and organizational decision maker. "Does this serve the vision?" is the test question, instead of "Who has power, what leverage do I have, where do I owe a favor, or where am I owed one?"
- Visionbuilding makes you smarter. It engages your whole mind—both brain hemispheres. You are more powerful when both your right and left brain are active and working together. The right brain is intuitive, creative, open-minded, and receptive, and it sees the big picture. The left brain is focused, logical, concrete, tough-minded, and linear. Whole-brain intelligence is the best intelligence there is.

- Visionbuilding comes with a free bonus—improvements in all areas of life. If you upgrade the electrical wiring in your house, all the lights and appliances work better. Visionbuilding is like that. The upgraded mindset and skills that build a vocational vision, for example, improve your physical, emotional, spiritual, and financial life and your relationships.
- Visionbuilding solves problems and prevents new ones. Albert Einstein is quoted as saying, "No problem can be solved from the same level of consciousness that created it." You need a new and better way of approaching it. The visionbuilders' system provides that way.
- Visionbuilders succeed without suffering. They experience stress-free, pain-free, struggle-free, burnout-free success. The "happy brain" principle and the "joy or nothing" practice teach you to operate from the right emotional state for success. That optimal state of mind for success is joy.
- Visionbuilders navigate from inner guidance, not from outer circumstances. You become more confident and sure-footed. People, places, and things that used to control you lose their power, because you trust your inner guidance above all else.
- Visionbuilders win without competing. Since only you can be best at your unique vision, you have no competition, and your success is assured.
- Great mental health is a visionbuilder's everyday experience. You are never confused or manipulated, and guilt is gone forever. Self-awareness and self-mastery ensure your peace of mind and well-being.
- As an entrepreneur or leader, you spend less of yourself and your resources, because visionbuilding is efficient.
- You will fulfill your natural instinct to create and contribute and be happy in the process.

Even the most excited and committed visionbuilder needs tools, because hidden fears can be relentless and because the rigors of sustained effort can offer an excuse to quit. Tools for self-mastery, self-awareness, and success mindset development are a big and important part of the visionbuilders' program.

To use the tools effectively, you need to know certain universal laws and principles, for two reasons: (1) you want to get them working in your favor, and (2) they will help establish the success mindset that you need, because, without the right mindset, self-sabotage will sink your vision.

Vision is a blueprint, a design of what the finished product will be. But blueprints themselves don't build buildings. That takes principles and tools and the skills to use them effectively. It's the same with building vision.

Successful visionbuilders have knowledge of the principles that affect their efforts, a well-developed intuitive sense, and solid "nuts and bolts" skills, such as planning, organizing, and budgeting. In corporate visionbuilding, a lack of knowledge can be an especially dangerous pitfall. Unless the organization makes sure that its systems, structures, and policies align with its vision, the vision will wither and die.

The visionbuilders' program includes all the essential elements: an authentic vision, self-mastery tools, foundation principles for a success mindset, and a step-by-step system of whole-brain intuitive and nuts-and-bolts skills that bring the vision into form. These elements are your recipe for panoramic success. Follow the recipe as this manual guides you, and you'll flunk out of Failure School for good.

Chapter 3

IT'S THE LAW

Laws That Make Visionbuilding Fast and Easy or Slow and Hard

Have you heard the saying "Ignorance of the law is no excuse"? The thing about laws is that they're in effect whether we know about them or not. As a kid, I was more girlie than tomboy, but still I'd launch myself off the porch into a pile of fall leaves or winter snow. Did I know about the law of gravity? Heck no, but I still rocketed down 7 feet every time. I never fell upward, and I couldn't change my mind midair. The law was the law, consistent and impartial.

Most of us eventually learn at least the fundamental laws of physics, biology, and the natural world. We are less likely to know the laws of how human beliefs create life experiences. But they are as important as gravity to your daily life and your visionbuilding. This chapter is about those laws.

The content and quality of your thoughts determine the content and quality of your life. The beliefs and attitudes you hold in your conscious and subconscious mind—your mindset—create your life experiences. That may trouble you, but keep an open mind and stay with me as we explore more about the power of your thoughts.

Do you name your cars? I have, for years. Don't ask me why, because I have no logical reason; it's just something I do. My

1980 full-size Mercedes was "Sherman," because it looked like a Sherman tank with leather seats and a silver paint job. Sherman was good to me, and I sold it for nearly $5,000 when the odometer hit 300,000 miles. My current Mercedes E320 is "George," named after my beloved Uncle George, who was as reliable, handsome, and solid as his namesake.

Between Sherman and George was "Guido," a 1994 E300 and my first black Mercedes. When I first saw it at the showroom, I had a flashback to the "Mafia cars" of my New York youth—long shiny black Mercedes with scary-looking guys inside. Because my 1950s white middle-class Protestant existence was pretty bereft of excitement, my young imagination often went into overdrive. Among my Irish, Polish, Jewish, and Italian friends, the Italians were the most exotic and glamorous to me, mainly because I imagined that their families were secretly connected to "THE Family"—whoa! The drama! The danger! I scared myself silly with the stories I made up about those guys and their Mercedes. In the dealer showroom that day, I laughed at myself, bought the car, and named it "Guido." I thought it was funny until . . .

The first accident was a parking lot fender bender. Didn't think much of it. Stuff happens, right? A few months later, a guy blazed through a yellow light and hit me. I wasn't hurt, but Guido spent a week in the body shop. There was more to come.

Our house was in a California canyon. The elevated front yard was banked by a 4-foot concrete wall, facing the sidewalk and extending the length of the driveway, which was at street level. My schedule meant that I often left Guido parked there rather than pull in and out of the garage all day. One Tuesday, a speeding car slammed into the wall. It missed Guido by inches, smashed the wall into rubble, and frayed my last nerve, as I watched from my home office window. It was as if Guido had dodged an assassin's bullet.

A question began to form in my mind. Could it be that naming the car "Guido," a name I associated with stereotypical 1960s

Mafioso, was somehow responsible for the continued violence to the car? Was the way I defined the car in my mind affecting outer circumstances? Could universal laws of cause-and-effect apply to human thought?

The final blow was another parking lot sideswipe, this time by a rental car full of foreign tourists in Santa Monica. In broken, excited English, they conveyed their wish to pay cash for the repairs, no paperwork, no police: "Don't tell rental company, we settle this outside of law for cash." The driver produced his driver's license and passport—both Italian. Can you guess his name? Of course you can—Guido.

What I have come to call "my Guido lesson" taught me a powerful law of life. Believe it or not and like it or not, there is an invisible cause-and-effect principle that rules our lives. Our beliefs, thoughts, and emotions form a blueprint or set of instructions that our mental energy carries out. Because the process is mostly subconscious, it looks like life happens to us instead of through us, or because of our subconscious instructions. Have you heard the expression "What you think about, you bring about"? Turns out it's true.

Here's how it worked in the Guido example (the car, not the Italian tourist). I had given my car a name that I unconsciously associated with violence and lawlessness. The association wasn't rational, but it stuck in my mindset nonetheless. That definition caused my subconscious mind to form a blueprint of Guido that was involved in violence and lawlessness. My subconscious thought energy fueled that blueprint into reality. It was as if I had given myself instructions—"OK, Margaret, make the blueprint real"—and then followed them. When the speeding car zoomed down our street, my subconscious mind made sure Guido was parked right in its path. It was likely the same process with the rest of poor Guido's story.

The cause-and-effect power of your mindset is both your best friend and your worst enemy. Understanding it and working in harmony with it mean that you get more of what you want and less of what you don't. Sadly, the reverse is true too. It works the same whether you believe it, use it, or ignore it. It's your choice.

This chapter describes that power in terms of laws. A law is a set of principles or rules. I use the term in the science or philosophy sense of invariable relationships that can be measured or are known instinctively. The laws of self-preservation and of supply and demand are examples. The visionbuilders' laws are the principles and rules about how your beliefs, thoughts, and emotions (mindset) create or hamper your success. The rest of the book teaches mindset mastery through the power of vision.

Where did I get these laws? I made them up! I discerned the concepts over time, as I worked with hundreds of visionbuilders. Observing the nature of their struggles and triumphs, I saw consistent patterns. Were there universal laws at work? I continued my field observations and began to study various sciences. I found relationships between the emerging laws of visionbuilding and established laws of physics, thermodynamics, psychology, biology, and systems science.

Even if you're not comfortable with the visionbuilders' laws and aren't sure they're true, at least imagine what your world would be like if they were!

The Laws of Visionbuilding

The Law of Vision Fulfillment

Systems science gives us some great clues about how a vision works. A system is a set of interacting elements that form a whole and a set of rules that governs behavior or structure. The solar system, digesting your lunch burrito, banking, and the software that generated these words are examples.

A basic law of systems science is that every action within a system triggers a reaction, called feedback. Feedback comes in two forms. One form accelerates the effect of the action and one modifies it according to rules of balance or homeostasis. If you're not into systems science, the terms reinforcing and balancing might be counterintuitive. A good way to understand them is this: reinforcing makes an action stronger, whereas balancing changes or ends it. The existence of a goal determines which kind of feedback is in charge and what happens. Here's how it all works.

Just about everyone has heard the piercing screech of feedback into a microphone. The speaker talks into the microphone, the sound bounces to a surface and back into the microphone, getting amplified as it does. Screech! The effects of reinforcing feedback make you cringe. If the speaker puts a hand over the microphone that stops the feedback, because the returning sound can't get back into the microphone to be amplified, so no screech. Balancing feedback saved the day.

Reinforcing feedback accelerates an existing trend. If you put a sailboat in the water, hoist the sails, then sit down with a beer and ignore them, what happens? The wind blows east, and your boat travels east; the wind blows south, and your boat heads south; a speedboat comes by and you're tossed around by its wake. The wind is the action, and the trends are the directions your boat moves with them. Nothing stops (or counteracts) the action-reaction cycle, so the trend accelerates. You change direction only when the wind does, getting banged around, drifting or traveling in a direction not of your choosing.

Another example of reinforcing feedback is falling off a cliff. The trend that is your descent accelerates, because no counteraction stops it. You plummet to the bottom of the ravine because nothing stopped the progression of your downward trend.

Balancing feedback occurs when there is a goal. (A vision is a goal—see where we're going with this?) Based on that goal, balancing feedback makes adjustments to close the gap between the goal and the current state. A goal changes everything. Let's say your goal is to reach the marina on the other side of the lake, east of where you launch your boat. You hoist your sails, and instead of kicking back with a beer, you take the wheel and steer east. With your goal in mind, you adjust your sails according to the direction and force of the wind. When the wind takes you off course, you balance that trend by steering your way to your destination. You don't change the trends—the wind actions—but you change your own actions in response to them, in order to achieve your goal.

A vision is a goal that functions in the same way. The law of vision fulfillment will seek to adjust your thoughts and actions to fulfill your vision. If you're straying from your vision, the law will act to refocus you. If you are overworking and overexerting your body, the law will find a way to stop you in your tracks so that you'll rest. If you need more money to create your vision, the law will find a way to provide it. (I knew you'd like that one. But remember, it's not passive. You still have to go where you're inwardly led and act as you're guided.)

The Law of Mindset Supremacy

You've probably heard the phrase "self-fulfilling prophesy." It means that your beliefs and subconscious thoughts (your mindset) create your reality. It has a longstanding foundation in social science. Forms of it can be found as far back as ancient Greece and India. It's still going strong in the modern world—in economics, psychology, medicine, and social sciences. It's been popularized the last few years as "the law of attraction."

Its defining incarnation in the twentieth century is the Thomas theorem. In 1928, W. I. Thomas said, "If men define situations as real, they are real in their consequences." In 1949, Robert K. Merton coined the term "self-fulfilling prophecy" in his book *Social Theory and Social Structure*.

In modern scientific research, the law shows up as the observer expectancy effect, in which researchers' mental biases cause them unconsciously to influence the outcome of an experiment. In medicine, it shows up as the placebo effect: what patients believe about a remedy becomes true for them, regardless of the objective truth about the remedy. Pills containing no medicine have cured patients who believed there was medicine in the pills.

A landmark study in the 1960s in the field of psychology was one of the first to validate the power of subconscious belief to create reality. Researchers Robert Rosenthal and Lenore Jacobson conducted double-blind experiments with schoolteachers and their students. Teachers were told that certain students were of exceptional ability and great promise.

At the study's end, those "exceptional" children performed significantly better than their peers. The startling fact was that they were not measurably smarter than their peers. The study showed that the teachers gave those they believed were "high-potential" children significantly more attention, encouragement, and praise. Controlling for measured intelligence and other factors, the independent variable was the teacher's behavior. The false belief that those students were exceptional came true because of the teacher's beliefs and resulting treatment of the students.

Rosenthal and Jacobson termed the phenomenon "the Pygmalion effect," after the Greek mythical character Pygmalion, who falls in love with a sculpture he created, believing that she is real. In the myth, the sculpture came to life. It's been shown again and again: beliefs, thoughts, and attitudes create reality.

Your mindset includes beliefs, attitudes, and thoughts that trigger emotions and make you act in a way that reinforces your mindset. Where you focus your energy determines the nature of the experience you create. It doesn't matter what you want or don't want. The object of your attention will show up in your experience.

When you fret over not getting a cold; you pretty much ensure that you'll get one. Why? You've focused your energy on the experience of having a cold, so subconsciously you're creating or attracting the experience, reinforcing the "I'm going to get a cold" belief that caused you to worry. Conversely, when you happily believe you are healthy, you can get caught in the rain, not eat right, and cheat yourself on sleep and still stay healthy. What you believe is what you experience.

The law of mindset supremacy is this: Your mindset creates your experiences. Every experience in your life you created, invited, attracted, expanded, promoted, or allowed. No exceptions. Your life circumstances are a direct reflection of your beliefs, thoughts, and emotions.

One of my students called this law "Margaret's most maddening truth." Can you see why? This law means you are never a victim, but always personally responsible. It's easier to lay blame for our problems on anything or anyone besides ourselves and harder to be personally responsible. I say the law of mindset supremacy is cause for celebration! Now we have the key to life as we desire it. In the words of Ernest Holmes, "Change your thinking, change your life." Think a new thought, instill a new belief, tell yourself a different story, and you change your life. By putting yourself consciously in charge of your thoughts, you become fully in charge of your life.

> # Margaret's
> # Most Maddening Truth:
>
> *"Every experience in your life you created, invited, attracted, expanded, promoted, or allowed. No exceptions."*

The Law of Mindset Mirroring

This law corresponds to the laws of biological science. An organism or a species is only capable of reproducing within its own kind. Genetics follows strict rules. Except for "designer farming" and the occasional mutation, organisms reproduce biological copies of themselves.

If you look in a mirror, you see an accurate reflection of your physical self. When you look at your life, you see an accurate reflection of your beliefs, attitudes, and emotions. Your mindset creates experiences that exactly mirror it. You always create precisely what's in your mindset. Your beliefs and emotions make the blueprint and then build an experience from that blueprint, exactly as it existed in your mind—a mirror. I subconsciously believed that my car Guido would live a life of violence and destruction—and it surely did.

If you plant peas in your garden, you get peas. Can't change your mind later and turn them into petunias. The law has been set in motion and fulfilled itself. You can't go to your garden, look at the peas, and say, "OK, now I want you to all turn into petunias." The peas will look back at you and say, "Look, here's the deal. We can't be petunias; we're peas! If you wanted petunias, you should have planted petunias!" Precisely. You reap what you sow. You change your life only by changing what you plant.

There's more to understand about how your emotional state shows up in the mirror of your life experiences. In Chapter 5, you'll learn that in creating your circumstances, your emotional state is even more powerful than your beliefs. You'll also learn skills to help you change detrimental emotions into better feelings that help build your vision.

The Law of Limits

In systems science, the law of system boundaries dictates that, in terms of cause and effect, a system can neither have an impact nor be affected by what's outside its boundaries. Every system has boundaries; it is one way in which a system is defined. You and I are systems, with boundaries that affect the scope of our influence. How those boundaries work is important for visionbuilders. Sometimes our boundaries overlap or intersect, but mostly they do not.

If I cut my finger, I wouldn't put a bandage on yours. Our physical bodies are separate systems; protecting your finger won't protect mine. Our beliefs and attitudes and actions work the same way. We affect our own lives; that's our greatest influence. Beyond that, we begin to get outside our system boundaries and our influence ends fast.

Let's consider your influence over others. You may have some if you and another person are part of a larger system—such as a family or a business. There's an area of intersection between the two systems where you interact and have influence. Because of the law of boundaries, it is never absolute; it's limited to that space of intersection. If you've ever tried to get your teenager to bend to your parental will, you're making my point for me. People create their own experiences because they are individual systems—with other interactions and influences besides you. (Kind of an ego punch, isn't it?) If politicians, lovers, psychotherapists, and parents had absolute control over others, we'd be living in, well, a very different world. You control your own life, but not all of life. On your very best day, your influence outside the boundaries of your own subsystem is limited and indirect.

Your mindset, however, is within your system boundaries, so, in mastering it, you exert increasing mastery over your life. Maybe you are miserable in a dead-end job. Change the content of that job? Nope—it's not within your system boundaries. Deciding that dead-end job is a fun way to learn more about dealing with the public? Yes. It's within your system boundaries and likely to improve the quality of your days. Of course, you could quit and find another job, but, as the saying goes, "wherever you go, there you are."

Let's consider the natural world. In my 18 years living in southern California, there were many earthquakes. Because I always had the conviction that I would never be injured in one, nor would my property ever be damaged, and because I never gave earthquakes a moment of worry (no focus of my thought energy), my subconscious never once placed me anywhere near one. But here's the important question: What if I worried that I would be in an earthquake? Would my subconscious thoughts create an earthquake to fulfill that belief? Do I have that power? Of course not. System boundaries are in force. Only nature creates earthquakes.[1] But what my subconscious mind could create would be my presence in the time and space of an earthquake. Earthquakes and other acts of nature happen; you don't personally create them, and you don't personally control them. You attract

---

1   To be technically correct, we'll concede exceptions for human interventions that stimulate natural events, such as seeding clouds to make rain and technology that affects the paths of hurricanes.

yourself to them—or not. Stuff happens. The natural world and other humans act as their own system boundaries allow. You, within your own system boundaries, have personal control over only two things: (1) where, when, and how to place yourself in time and space, and (2) what your personal experience will be—according to the beliefs and attitudes in your mindset.

The Law of Personal Evolution

This law has its foundation in biology, specifically in Darwin's theory of evolution and laws of natural selection. Evolution is a process in which something changes into a form that is more suited to its environment. According to an idea that has been popularly termed survival of the fittest, Darwin taught that there are natural changes—mutations—in genes. As organisms reproduce, nature makes selections among them. The organisms best suited to their current environment survive and reproduce. Their lineage continues, whereas that of those less suited doesn't.

If you were a light-colored moth during the industrial revolution, you were in trouble. The increasing pollution made the surfaces of buildings where you hung out sooty and dark. You were easily visible and an easy target for your predators. Your darker-colored cousins had an advantage. They blended in better, and predators had to work harder to find them. That advantage affected their genetic coding, so that, over time, there were fewer light-colored moths and more darker-colored moths. That's natural selection.

Biological adaptations happen in response to environmental changes and challenges, always advancing toward advantages. If you were a tourist roaming the globe 200,000 years ago, you might meet both *Homo neanderthalis* and *Homo sapiens*. Most scientists agree that both were around then. We Homo sapiens are here, and homo neanderthalis are not. About 30,000 years ago, we became the only folks around. It's still an open question whether we evolved as parallel species and they died off while we continued, or whether the two interbred until our genetic traits dominated. Whatever happened, it happened because of superior environmental adaptability. Genetics advances toward the advantages.

Is what's true for moths, Neanderthals, and Homo sapiens true for visionbuilders? Yes. Your mindset works like a genetic code, only better. Your biological coding determines your physiology (including brain attributes that make mindset possible). Mindset is the belief system that generates your life experiences. It's part of who you are as an organism, similar to your eye color and hair texture. But eye color and hair texture are fixed, whereas your mindset isn't. Your mindset is the mental coding that causes you to think and act a certain way. What makes it better than a genetic code is that, if your mindset isn't supporting your vision, you can change it—today. It doesn't take generations to adapt to environmental challenges. That in-the-moment mindset evolution potential is a powerful advantage for visionbuilders.

You control the evolution of your mindset by changing the beliefs that don't give you an environmental advantage into ones that do. Biology is destiny, but mindset is destiny only if you let it be. Developing a population of light-colored moths or superior humans takes generations, but you can adapt your mindset right now.

What kind of environmental challenges and advantages affect human mindset and how do we know the right adaptations to make? Let's look to the story of a visionbuilder named Vic. The events are over 10 years old, but they represent an enduring good example of mindset evolution. Vic had a struggle with money, earning it and then losing it through poor investments or giving it away to anyone with a story of need. No matter how much Vic earned, it was soon gone. In our environment, it's an advantage to have access to money, and, if you don't, you're at an environmental disadvantage—like light-colored moths and Neanderthals. Vic's environmental disadvantage was created by a mindset attribute rather than by a biological one—thus it could be changed right away.

The visionbuilders' process produced the "aha" that changed everything—"Wow, I realize that I believe if I have a lot of money I will do harm with it!" Huh? It was immediately clear to Vic that his belief made no sense and could easily be changed. The better, more advantageous belief for living in Vic's environment was clear too: "I do only beneficial things with my money." Vic made an evolutionary mindset change in a matter of minutes.

How did Vic know about the more advantageous belief? He didn't have to avoid predators or fight for evolutionary dominance. Fortunately, we humans can learn without that kind of feedback. Our human intelligence helps us see where the finger of Darwin points. Like Vic, we often discern the most advantageous mindset component in a flash of insight. When insight doesn't come in a flash, we use our intelligence to deduce from our environment what might work better. Vic might have chosen to observe people with healthy money attitudes, learned those attitudes, and then chosen to adopt them. Your goal of a vision will lead you to your next step in mindset evolution.

Becoming a Law-Abiding Visionbuilder

The visionbuilders' skills you'll learn in upcoming chapters have the previously described laws as their foundation. As you learn and practice the laws of vision fulfillment, mindset supremacy, mindset mirroring, limits, and personal evolution, you'll validate them for yourself with your own experiences as a successful visionbuilder. Use these guidelines, tips, and perspectives about the laws to support your skill development.

Invest to Guarantee Your Maximum ROI

ROI is a business term meaning return on investment. To decide whether to develop product A or product B (investment), companies calculate the projected profits and other benefits (return). As a visionbuilder, you want the maximum ROI from your efforts working with the laws and the visionbuilders' skills. You want to invest yourself wisely. Where is your best ROI?

Life happens in the invisible realm first—in your conscious and subconscious mind—and then becomes visible as your life experiences. Doesn't it make sense to spend most of your efforts working within your mind? That means working more on your beliefs and attitudes and less on outer circumstances. Is someone giving you a hard time at work? Look within first for the beliefs and attitudes behind your reaction and—only based on what you learn—take external action. Your mindset has caused you to define their actions as "a hard time," and your mindset can cause you to define it differently. It's your perception of someone else's behavior that causes you to suffer. You can chose to ignore it, perceive it differently, or be neutral about it. It all happens in your mind. That's the best place to take action and the best place to look for guidance on any external action that might be needed. If you aren't making the progress you want, or you feel stuck, take the ROI approach. Your greatest ROI comes from inner investment first, outer action last.

Remember too, that you can never influence what has already happened. You have no power there. You can only create anew— that is where your power is. You create anew from new beliefs, attitudes, and thoughts.

Imagine Your Way to Success

Maybe you've heard of or even done experiments about using your imagination. I was once at a seminar where we were asked to imagine a lemon—its bright yellow color, its thick nubby skin, and its pungent sour taste. Next, we were told to imagine biting into that lemon—through the bitter skin into the cold, tart, sour fruit. Every person in the room made the same puckered face! We could taste that lemon! Our minds couldn't tell the difference between imagined and real.

That's the key to the power of imagination: your subconscious can't tell the difference between imagined and real. That's why affirmations and visualizations work, and it's also why your beliefs about a person or a situation or a relationship can cause you to react as though they were real.

Let's say you have a coworker named Joe whom you think you can't trust. You heard some gossip that caused you to form a negative attitude about him. You'll reflect that "Joe can't be trusted" attitude in your dealings with him, looking for reasons to be suspicious. If Joe forgets a meeting with you or shows up late, you'll decide, "Aha, he did that for some sneaky malicious reason!" If Joe accidentally spills coffee on your desk, you'll decide, "Aha, he's trying to drown my monthly report and get me fired!" If Joe walks you to your car, you'll decide, "Aha, he's trying to see which car is mine so he can slash my tires when I'm not looking!" The way you treat poor Joe, based on your beliefs about him, is the same as puckering up your face because of an imaginary lemon.

But you're a smart visionbuilder. You understand the role of your mindset in the drama, and so you decide to change your suspicious thoughts into thoughts of trust. Whenever you think of Joe or you're with him, you intentionally imagine his innocent motives, honesty, and trustworthiness. (Remember "inspansion" from Chapter 2? You expand a new idea or belief within your mind until it shows up in reality.) That imagined belief will create a new attitude toward Joe. Whether or not the gossip about him was true, your new trusting attitude will change your side of the relationship. The new Joe whom you experience in your mind is a trustworthy coworker. And, because people's behavior has been known to change based on how they're treated, Joe may in fact become that ideal guy you have imagined.

Watch out for Blind Spots

You understand the power of your beliefs and the laws that create your reality. You know you are hardwired to be happy, productive, and at peace. Yet perhaps your life doesn't always reflect what you know. You have blind spots. We all do. They can trip you up in your visionbuilding journey.

If you want to locate your blind spots, look at your life. Blind spots leave trails. Look at the areas where you are not feeling fulfilled, successful, or happy. Those are where a belief or attitude is diminishing your power. You can see the result, but you can't see the underlying belief because your conscious mind is blind to it.

Let's say you have a blind spot having to do with supply: you believe in lack instead of abundance. That subconscious belief might show up as financial lack, lack of time, energy, or creativity, lack of fulfilling relationships or good health. You will make up good, logical reasons and excuses for your lacks, and maybe you blame outside circumstances. You may not be able to see the underlying belief that's causing them. But it's there.

Through your regular practice of stillness, self-questioning, and observing your life, your blind spots will show themselves. The same practices will also guide you to create better beliefs and better experiences. More about these in Chapters 5 and 6.

Have Better Conversations

Do you have a tendency to play "Ain't it awful"? It's a common game. You get your friends, family, coworkers, and anyone you can convince to agree with your complaints and even elaborate on them. Have you noticed that your greatest complaints keep showing up again and again? That's because you keep fueling them with your energy. Convincing other people to add their energy to the mix fuels your own problems even more. Your combined energy extends and intensifies their lives. Soon, everyone you know agrees that your life is awful. And so it is.

I've noticed that my complaints go away when I stop feeding them. I've noticed something else too. I enjoy conversations about a vision much more than a whining session. They just feel better.

Having uplifting, positive, creative conversations is a great use of the visionbuilders' laws. Enough of these conversations and soon everyone you know agrees that your life is wonderful. And so it is.

Ask Better Questions

When life isn't going our way, it's natural to ask why. Humans are curious by nature. We want to know why people act how they act or why a circumstance is what it is. We want to believe that knowing will make things better. It's hard to imagine solving a problem without a few why questions.

Why questions tempt us with understanding and intellectual and emotional satisfaction. Answers feel good, but they don't necessarily solve your problem or build your vision. You still must make sense of the answer in the context of your goal—more analysis—and with no guarantee that it will apply. When I worked in management consulting, we dreaded clients getting lost in "analysis paralysis"— endless why questions leading them further and further from solutions. Even the field of psychology has moved away from extensive analysis and toward goal-driven behavior change.

What questions offer an objective basis for change. They keep you focused on a current reality—what it means to your goals and what needs adjusting: "What are the circumstances? What, if anything, should I do about them?"

Next time you are tempted to solve a problem by asking why, try instead the visionbuilders' WD-40® questions: like the famous product, WD-40®, these kinds of questions can unstick anything. You'll find a full explanation, instructions, and examples in Chapter 6, but I want you to have the questions now as part of your guidelines for working with the laws.

The visionbuilders' WD-40® questions:

- What more is there for me to see? To be? Or to set free?
- What is my highest vision for right now?
- Does this serve my vision—yes or no?

It's best to work with introspective processes, such as the WD-40® questions, in silence and stillness. See the stillness practice in Chapter 6. It's a form of meditation that I think you'll find comfortable and easy and with the same benefits as the more formal or religious ones.

Stop Fixing and Start Creating

There is a powerful difference between fixing and creating. It's a distinction that helps us become better visionbuilders. Let's say I have a bad situation at work, maybe my boss always says no to my suggestions. If I try to fix the situation, here's what happens. I continue to affirm that I am living in the middle of a problem; I am holding in my mind the thought "I have a problem." I own it and I live in it. What does that get me? I continue living in the problem, because I have given it my continued attention. I have fed and nourished it, and it will thrive.

If instead I call it my current perception (a changeable belief instead of a permanent truth)—"I currently believe my boss always says no to every suggestion I make"—I recognize this as just my current perception. By thinking of it this way, now I am free to continue to feed it or to starve it. I can starve it by giving it no attention and instead creating a positive belief, "My boss listens to my suggestions, and together we make great progress." Now I have a positive direction to move in. Now I am creating a new experience, not fixing a problem.

Adopt a Patience Perspective

Sometimes creating your dreams happens in pieces and increments, and progress seems excruciatingly slow. Success grows as understanding grows. It's important to remember that your inner growth rate determines the speed of your success. Your rate of inner investment determines your outer rate of return. Remember this whenever you get frustrated with the outer world for not serving up your wants fast enough. And—this is really important—resist the urge to force outer events to move faster. Stay on the path and keep doing the inner work, where you know your greatest ROI is. Soon you'll notice the outer world becoming a faster delivery system for your dreams.

Be Kind to Yourself

In case you're inclined to beat yourself up, because you've created some experiences you wish you hadn't, realize that you subconsciously choose those experiences in order to learn, grow, and evolve. The best part of you is always seeking a better way of being. It's part of your innate hardwiring for success—continually becoming the person who can create and live your next big dreams. Please remember this, and give yourself a break when you think you've made a mess of things. Instead, be grateful that you are constantly evolving, celebrate your courage, and ask yourself, "What am I learning from this experience?"

Chapter 4

A BLANK CHECK TO FUND YOUR VISION

"It is your fears, not your flaws, that keep you from financial freedom"

Margaret Shepherd:
Cash and Consciousness: 21 Days to Prosperity.

In the Middle Ages, if you couldn't pay your bills you were locked away in debtor's prison. You were deprived of freedom and any chance of prosperity. How did that make sense? Lock you up if you can't pay your debts, so you have no chance to earn money, plus the government pays your keep at taxpayers' expense. Samuel Johnson, in his 1758 essay titled "Debtor's Prison," said, "The prosperity of a people is proportionate to the number of hands and minds usefully employed. . . . The confinement, therefore of any man in the sloth and darkness of a prison is a loss to the nation, and no gain to the creditors."

Old Samuel got it right, and you would think that, by the twenty-first century, we'd have evolved beyond such nonsense. Not yet. Today we have a modern debtor's prison. It's not built of bricks and mortar, but of misguided beliefs. It exists in your mind. It is at least as harmful to your well-being and as detrimental to your society as the medieval version.

In a throwback to centuries past, modern cultures still separate God and money. (Because this comes from certain religious beliefs and is about the concept of God, I am not making the usual substitution of the term *the Universe.*) We learn to seek wealth—"money is good"—and we learn that poverty is holy—"money is bad." These conflicting messages aren't just philosophical confusions. They cause real trouble in real life. Our credit card debt crisis is an example. We buy material things and expensive experiences to enhance our lives (proving money is good), and our impossible debt provides the noble suffering of poverty (proving money is bad). We operate from these conflicting messages, and the cycle of suffering continues unless its underlying premise changes.

Visionbuilding is another example. The single underlying reason every person on the planet isn't a successful visionbuilder is fear. The most common answer to the question "Why haven't you created that vision yet?" is "I can't afford it. It would cost a fortune. Where would I get the money?" The second most common answer, "I don't have the time," is another form of the poverty mindset you'll learn about in this chapter. Money, time, opportunities, resources of any sort are all subject to the same mindset of fear of lack. They are different versions of the same poverty mindset. But there's good news. Change one, they all change. You get a lot of leverage for your effort.

The supply of universal energy is infinite and inexhaustible; your only limit is your beliefs. Your cultural programming has instilled negative and limiting messages about money in your subconscious. Those messages run your life from a seat of invisible power in your head.

Poverty-creating messages that you may have internalized from Failure School and otherwise include the following: "Money is the root of all evil." "A fool and his money are soon parted." "It's harder for a rich man to get into Heaven than for a camel to fit through the eye of a needle." You can probably add to the list without much effort.

There are troublemaker messages about occupations and poverty steeped in our collective consciousness too. Starving artists, poor schoolteachers, impoverished clergy, and dedicated but poor social workers are all victims of our collective beliefs. The people who live these stereotypes have absorbed them, consciously or not.

These messages about money and occupation can cause visionbuilders two problems. First, it's just not true that any occupation inherently creates poverty or prosperity. It is the mindset of individuals, not their occupation that creates or resists prosperity. You can find the fabulously wealthy working in any field and subsistence workers in any field too. Doctors are supposed to be rich, yet I personally know several who barely get by. Artists are supposed to be poor, yet I was in the seminary with a multimillionaire artist. They weren't exceptions; they just had a different money mindset.

Believing in the inherent financial consequences of an occupation can prevent you from considering it for yourself. If I am inspired to be a social worker and have the natural desire to thrive financially, I am faced with a tough choice. If I follow my heart's desire, I will impoverish myself. If instead I choose to work in a field that is not my heart's desire because I believe it is my only chance to prosper, I will remain unfulfilled and unexpressed. How can I pursue my vision if it leads me to such a lose-lose crossroads? I want a win-win result.

In the institutional religions that shape our culture, business often has a low reputation. Business has to do with making money, and the rift between God and money is ancient. God and money are separate and at odds. We must be poor to be holy; money is "dirty," the "root of all evil." Clergy take vows of poverty. Business is synonymous with corruption. Sunday is about God, and Monday is about money.

This disparity traps us in an impossible choice between the spiritual and the material. We want to be godly, and yet we want physical well-being, material comfort, creative expression, human innovation. and the joys of life that business provides and money buys.

Our beliefs about business and money affect our work lives, too. Dozens of people in my "Cash and Consciousness" prosperity program couldn't let themselves prosper doing work that they loved, so they kept a "day job" they hated so they could pay the bills. Their hidden logic was that, if your heart's desire is godly, and money is not, it is somehow immoral to receive money for working at your heart's desire; money can only come from unholy work—a hated "day job." Following similar logic, a church ministry I was hired to help prosper had to confront its collective horror—at considering itself a business—before it could move forward.

Is it the universe's intent that we chose between the spiritual and the material? Are business and money inherently evil? Is our suffering a test, and, if so, where the heck is the answer sheet?

Smart visionbuilders like you know that there is always a solution. They know to let go of the false belief that poverty or prosperity exists anywhere besides in your own mind. It is your consciousness that creates your abundance, not your occupation. Your prosperity comes from what's within you, not what's outside of you.

A Healthier Money Mindset

Visionbuilders adopt a healthier way to think about God and money. Money is God or the universe in action, providing for every requirement of your every vision. Money exists to supply human existence and creativity.

Your Supply

Money is supply, and supply is universal energy. You attract or repel money as you do any other form of energy—food, love, opportunities, human connections, ideas. You create your supply from your mindset, not by chasing it in the material world. The material world is the result, not the source. The source is the universe, partnering with you to create your heart's desires. The universe provides the inspiration and resources, including money, and you provide the human labor. When you think about it that way, it's a pretty good deal, isn't it?

"Cash follows creativity, not craving" is a quote from my book *Cash and Consciousness*. Here's what it means. Let's say you have the following thought: "If only I had more money, I could get a better car, and then my life would be perfect. But my salary is so puny I'll never save enough for the down payment, let alone the monthly payments. I really, really, really want more money." Remember the universal laws of visionbuilding (Chapter 3). If you crave money, it means you believe you don't have it and that you feel powerless to create it. Think about that a minute. When you tell the universe "I want," the law, being literal, gives you back exactly what you ordered—more of the experience of wanting. Its response is "OK, what you say is what you get. You ordered wanting, you get wanting, exactly as ordered. Makes no difference to me." It's like the Burger King® commercial says, "Have it your way."

You can see how the mindset of wanting creates more of itself. You get to drive your old rattletrap car until you change the order that your thoughts created. Remember that money exists as the universe's blank check for human creativity. Let's look again at your desire for money for a new car. If instead you made that desire about creativity instead of craving, what might it be? Perhaps it would be this: "I chose to create my perfect car. I create it in my mind exactly as I desire it to be and trust that it is coming into being. It is a brand-new black mini-SUV hybrid with a GPS, high-end music system, tan leather, and it has the highest fuel economy and safety rating. It is a joy to drive, and I feel good every time I'm in it. The money to pay for it is already available to me, and I choose to accept it now." With this thought, you have given the universe a completely different order, haven't you? You'll get a different result—your desired new car. Isn't that better than more craving?

Speaking of that new car, have you ever felt guilty desiring something material? Maybe you should give your money to the poor or save it for a rainy day instead. If you have, that guilt is likely coming from those poverty mindset cultural messages stuck in your subconscious. Although it is never smart to spend beyond your current means—and successful visionbuilders are good money stewards—it is smart to spend on what you desire, free of guilt. It takes a healthy money mindset.

Have faith in your perpetual ability to earn money, trust that the universe provides for your authentic desires, believe in your good financial stewardship, and take the steps to be a good money manager. Spend consciously, thoughtfully, and with joy—never guilt. If you think that new car you want (and can afford) is selfish, consider that your purchase is supporting the families of the dealership team, the production plant, the design engineers, assembly line workers, the restaurant where the workers buy lunch, the park where they take their kids, and the supermarket and mall where they shop. You are not just buying yourself a car; you are helping support people's lives and well-being.

Here is something else worth knowing as you grow into a healthier money mindset. All successful people are successful because they are working to create whatever is their passion, never because they are working to create money. Money is the means, not the goal. The vision is the goal. This is how the universe is set up, and it's a great system. It ensures that creativity inspires our lives and that, in its pursuit, we grow and serve each other. Money is provided to support our creativity and flows to it in a natural and effortless way if we let it.

You are here to create, and the universe supports your creativity. Creating goods and services is the nature of human society. Prosperity is your birthright, your natural destiny. It is blocked only by the subconscious belief that it is bad—somehow ungodly.

Come back into your inborn alignment with the universe's intention that you prosper, create, consume, manage, and love money and the goods and services it makes possible. Prosperity is yours to accept with ease. Train yourself to be vigilant for old beliefs, and do an immediate U-turn when you notice them. It takes some dedication, but the payoff is huge. You stop being an unwitting inmate of your own debtor's prison. Change your mind and thrive.

Keep in mind that changing your mindset and behavior is a process, not an event. Remember that emotions and other variables affect even your most dogged efforts and that a compelling vision is a powerful change accelerator.

The Poverty-Prosperity Self Test in this chapter will help you understand your current relationship with money and where you have work to do. Also, if you find you require a better money mindset, get a copy of my *Cash and Consciousness* e-book or any good program that teaches you the spiritual metaphysics of money. If you need this extra training, you must get it because you must have a healthy money mindset to build your vision.

Self-Test 1: Money Beliefs Exercise

Prosperity is the natural order of the universe, your birthright, essential to expressing your true self and giving your gifts to the world. If you have strayed from your natural prosperity, it is because you have accepted some false beliefs and let yourself be controlled by them. Your ego has hooked you into living in darkness instead of in light. Seeing what those beliefs might be is the first step to replacing them with healthier ones. This self-test will give you a simple awareness of what you believe and point you to what beliefs you may want to change.

The first statements are about your money beliefs right now. Use your intuition to reveal the truth to your conscious mind. Notice there is no scale or rating system. This is not a mental exercise, but an intuitive one. Pay attention to your first reaction. Does it seem true about you? Most of us have absorbed these beliefs from our culture, and even a small belief in any of them means they are in your subconscious mind where they are probably causing trouble. Getting free of them will create your prosperity.

Money Beliefs

Notice how you react to these statements. Which ones seem true for you now?

1. Money is the root of all evil.
2. To be holy I have to be poor.
3. The "pie" is limited; if I have more than somebody else, they will have that much less.
4. To have money I must work very hard and sacrifice much.
5. It is evil to want money; I should be humble and want no rewards for my efforts.
6. Truly intelligent, talented, and spiritual people are "above" money.
7. People who have a lot of money usually got it deceitfully, maybe illegally, but for sure at the expense of the poor.
8. If I have a lot of money, I shouldn't act like it; I shouldn't spend it flamboyantly or too freely.
9. It is important to save for a rainy day, sock it away because "you never know . . ."
10. "A penny saved is a penny earned."
11. "A fool and his money are soon parted."
12. It's OK to spend money on my dependents, family, or friends but selfish to spend it on myself.
13. If I had a lot of money, I would never have time to enjoy it; it would be a big responsibility and a hassle to manage.
14. And . . . add more that occur to you here.

Reflection

Reflect on the Money Beliefs Exercise. Observe your energy and your emotions and reflect on how you felt.

1. Which ones are the most powerful for you? Past and present, notice where your energy goes.
2. For those you no longer believe in, why not? How has life changed since you changed this belief?
3. For those you still believe in, what is their opposite? What could you believe instead?
4. How could your life be different if you believed the opposite?
5. Are you willing to believe the opposite? Why, or why not?

As you begin to adopt healthier money beliefs, it's important not to condemn your existing beliefs. To condemn is to give power and energy to what you don't want, which causes it to grow and thrive. The key is not to feed the beliefs that you want to extinguish. If you are holding the belief in your mind "I am terrible with money" and you get angry with yourself for that belief or struggle against it—you make it stronger! You have informed the universe, "I am terrible with money," even more strongly, and the universe—which always creates your reality from your beliefs—serves up an even stronger experience of "being terrible with money."

Self-Test 2: Poverty-Prosperity Mindset

Use this self-test to learn more about the inner world from which you experience the outer world of money. Whatever you find, take heart. That self-understanding is moving you toward the prosperity that is your natural state.

This is not a test that will give you an exact measurement. It is designed to give you a baseline sense of your prosperity consciousness and direct you to your biggest growth opportunities. Isn't it great to learn where you need to spend your efforts?

As you read the lists that define Poverty Consciousness and Prosperity Consciousness, ask yourself "Is that always, sometimes, or never me?" Write an A, S, or N in the space after the item.

Poverty Mindset

1. I am not clear on what I want to be, or do, or have.

   _____

2. I avoid responsibility for my failure or success. _____

3. I practice procrastination, or "analysis paralysis."

   _____

4. I don't feel deserving or worthy. _____

5. I have only limited curiosity. _____

6. I have only limited imagination or vision. _____

7. I often am hoarding, tightfisted, or a "prophet of doom."

   _____

8. I don't enjoy spending money on myself. _____

9. I feel guilty when I have money and guilty when I don't.

   _____

10. I have difficulty in receiving. _____

11. I lack excitement or enthusiasm for life. _____

12. I work at jobs I don't like just for the money. _____

Prosperity Mindset

1. I have enthusiastic clarity, a vision, single-minded focus.

   _____

2. I take full responsibility for all that happens to me.

   _____

3. I take focused, timely, and energetic movement toward my desires. _____

4. I have solid self-esteem; I believe in my own value.

   _____

5. I have boundless interest in life. _____

6. I have expansive, creative thoughts, wild ideas, a great imagination. _____

7. I operate from the awareness of unlimited supply. _____

8. My self-respect and self-valuing requires spending money on me. _____

9. Guilt is simply not an applicable emotion—not on my radar screen! _____

10. High self-worth makes it easy for me to receive. _____

11. I am an active, enthusiastic participant and lover of life. _____

12. I apply myself to work that brings me joy and fully uses my talents. _____

Reflection

As you contemplate your answers, focus on your "Always" and "Sometimes" responses. You have work to do there. Promise me you won't spend even one minute analyzing why you hold those beliefs. That will only strengthen them, because you feed them your thought energy. Instead, work to plant healthier money beliefs in your subconscious. Find the opposites of your "Always" and "Sometimes" poverty belief's in the Prosperity Consciousness list and get to work using them as affirmations. Speak them to yourself frequently, write them, do whatever you can to make them real to you. See the Anchoring Skill in Chapter 6 for how to use affirmations effectively. Soon you'll be living in the abundance you desire and deserve.

Part II

The Model

Chapter 5

THE SUCCESS TRIANGLE

I can always tell when visionbuilders have lost their way, because they suffer. They talk about their suffering, instead of reporting events objectively or sharing insights and growth opportunities. They speak of loss or being victimized. They blame. They judge. They're angry. They just plain suffer. I listen between the lines and can tell they feel powerless. They have forgotten who they are—powerful creative geniuses with infinite resources. Do you know that is who you are?

I've learned that, whenever I am seeking success, I must change in some way. My world does not change unless and until I do. I don't always like it, but I know I can't create what I want otherwise. Both my inner landscape and my outer actions have to be different, or my life won't be different. The principle is that your current mindset can only create more of the same experiences. You keep sending the same mental emotional signals that recreate your current circumstances. Success requires inner change. The Success Triangle helps you make it.

The Visionbuilders' Success Triangle

The visionbuilders' success triangle is your success blueprint. It's a how-to model of the three "gottahaves" that build vision. At the center of the triangle is vision, the engine that powers success. Chapters 2 and 9 are devoted exclusively to vision, so we'll focus now on the triangle's three sides. But first, I want to remind you of two principles that are key to vision, the center and focus of the success triangle:

The Right Vision for Right Now

Anything less won't inspire you to make the necessary mindset and action changes. Remember our definition of vision: an imagined ideal experience you want more than you fear change. The right vision for right now is compelling, authentic, and heartfelt. It passes all your objective tests and feels right in your bones. That's because it's in the area of life—personal, business, health, whatever—that's most important to you right now. The right vision for right now is the one that's so exciting and compelling that you just gotta live it!

Clear and Vivid

Clarity is crucial because the universe always says yes. The universal laws that govern vision are literal, impersonal, and they won't fill in the blanks of your incomplete intention. If you have only a fuzzy intention of abundance, you might get an abundance of problems! Or, if you vaguely want more customers, you might get more customers from hell! It's always worth the effort to determine the specific details of your desires. The more vivid your vision is in your imagination, the more it stimulates positive emotions, and the more likely you are to be in its hot pursuit.

The Success Triangle Sides

Self-mastery means command of thoughts, words, and deeds to make sure actions match intentions. Self-mastery controls your thoughts and emotions so that self-sabotage doesn't stand a chance. Self-mastery manages what stimulates your mind, matches mindset, actions, and vision, and keeps you focused on the prize. If you're not working toward self-mastery, you'll be stuck in your default life, instead of enjoying the success you want and deserve.

Success mindset means establishing beliefs that consistently create success. Inner beliefs make or break your power. With a success mindset, you are operating from beliefs, thoughts, and emotions that create success. Those old Failure School lessons may still be there in your subconscious, but the process of establishing a healthier mindset will eventually cause them to fade. They wither and die once they're no longer stimulated by your attention.

Whole-brain skills mean using both brain hemispheres to discover a right vision for right now and bring it into form. Whole-brain skills combine logic and intuition to make you your most powerful. Logic helps you evaluate facts and data, and intuition gives you access to your inner wisdom. Visionbuilders trust their inner voice so much that they say yes to it even when their logical mind is screaming no!

VISIONBUILDERS SUCCESS TRIANGLE

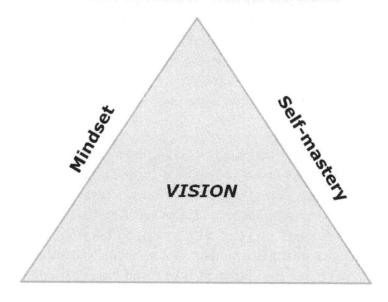

Whole-brain Skills

Success Triangle Center: A Clear Authentic Vision

A vision represents your highest ideal for any topic in human experience, a magnetic blueprint that attracts its own fulfillment. In a practical sense, a vision is an imagined ideal experience you want more than you fear change. If you skipped to this chapter, be sure to read the full discussion of vision in Chapter 2 before you move on to the visionbuilders' skills.

A clear authentic vision is your truest path to success, so it's always worth the effort. But it isn't always easy to come by. Contemplating a vision can bring up a lot of subconscious "stuff" and cause confusion and fears to steal your peace of mind. Sometimes people worry that the vision they see isn't real—maybe it's the wrong one, or not good enough, or maybe they don't have what it takes to create it. A clear authentic vision comes from connecting with your inner wisdom, the part of you that finds a "knowing, in your bones, what can or must be done."

Getting a clear vision is not rocket science. It is a process you can learn to use effectively and easily if you keep focused and keep your fears under control. Chapter 9, The Vision Discovery Process, helps you find a vision and shows you how to tell the real deal from imposters.

A clear compelling vision doesn't guarantee success and certainly doesn't immunize against challenges, but it does immunize you against suffering. Vision prevents suffering because the positive emotions you feel about your vision dissolve fears and false beliefs—including the belief that you have to suffer to succeed. As you begin to develop a success mindset, you begin to enable inevitable success in what matters most—your vision. You thrive instead of suffer.

Success Triangle Side One:
The Visionbuilders' Success Mindset

Your mindset is the set of beliefs you have accumulated during your years of living, including those old Failure School lessons we met in Chapter 1. Those beliefs cause certain attitudes that trigger various emotions as you go about your life. How do you know what's in your mindset?

Knowing your mindset content can be difficult, because studies have shown that we are conscious of about only about 5% of our brain activity—95% happens below our awareness, subconsciously. But your life provides clues about your mindset. Even though it might seem like amateur psychology, you can connect the dots with confidence, because you can verify your guesses. You guess at what mindset beliefs might be causing trouble, and then you can change your thoughts, based on your guesses. Then watch what happens.

If you're an overcontrolling type, for example, you can surmise that you might believe the world is a threatening place. Work to change that belief, and see if being flexible becomes easier. What's it like to go with the flow instead of trying to control things? If you tend to hoard like a pack rat, maybe you believe in scarcity. Work to change that belief, and see if you can give away or discard some belongings without having an anxiety attack. If you're generous of heart and wallet, perhaps you believe in an abundant universe. That's one you won't want to change, because it makes for a good life. You get the idea. Wherever you're suffering in your visionbuilding, there's a hidden belief to be changed.

Best-selling novelist Michael Crichton tells a story about his medical school years in his book *Travels*. He and his intern pals were bored, because nearly the whole surgical floor was filled with heart attack patients. Although a heart attack is pretty dramatic for the patient, apparently it's not the most exciting challenge for doctors-in-training. Hoping to liven up patient rounds, he decided he'd ask a different question from the usual checklist of symptoms. He asked instead, *"Why did you have a heart attack?"*

The responses shook him to his core and changed his entire view of medicine. First, every patient had an immediate answer. It was as if they had been asking themselves that question and waiting for a doctor smart enough to ask it. Second, every single patient reported a psychological or emotional reason. Nobody said it was too much bacon and too little exercise. They gave answers such as the following: *"I lost my job and my pension." "I want a divorce, and I feel guilty." "My daughter wants to marry someone of a different race."*

The astounded Crichton took his findings to the chief of medicine, who responded with a story of his own. He once was hospitalized with a slipped disc precisely when he had to reject a paper written by a close colleague. He understood that the slipped disc had postponed facing an unpleasant circumstance, and he saw a clear cause and effect.

Although you can't be precisely sure of the content of your mindset, you can be sure it's affecting your life experiences. Through this experience, Crichton began to understand what every successful visionbuilder understands: your mindset and emotions create your reality. In every area of your life, your skills, contacts, education, and intelligence all get trumped by your mindset and emotions. That's why visionbuilders focus first on the right mindset. We know that if we don't get that right, the rest is wasted energy.

Here's a question that might give you some interesting insights. Ask yourself a version of *"Why did I have a heart attack?"* Ask *"What is my greatest desire right now, and what mindset, beliefs, and thoughts are keeping me from it?"* See what comes up. If you're honest with yourself (it's just you and me, and I won't tell), your answer can lead you to inner changes that can create a watershed of positive outer results.

Vision-Mindset Congruence

No matter how much you want your business or personal vision, if your mindset doesn't line up with that vision, you will fail. Intention-mindset congruence is crucial. If you've ever experienced self-sabotage, you've experienced that lack of congruence—your conscious intention is sabotaged by something in your unconscious mindset.

For example, let's say you have a vision of becoming a financial planner, confidently guiding clients to financial well-being, but you have an inner belief that you won't be credible until you yourself become wealthy. Your lack of intention-mindset congruence will sabotage your efforts. Your belief will keep you stuck until it changes. You'll have one foot on the gas and one foot on the brake. What happens when one foot is zooming you forward and the other screeching you to a stop? Nothing! You're stuck. You spend a lot of energy, exhaust yourself, and get nowhere. That's what happens when your mindset and intention aren't aligned.

If you want to change your life, you have to change your mind—from the thoughts that hold you back to those that build success. A belief that success requires suffering will make you approach everything from that point of view. As you try to succeed in anything, you will subconsciously create, attract, or accept suffering, because that seems natural to you. You miss the success that is right in front of you, because it seems too easy. You haven't suffered enough. So you'll suffer and suffer and suffer some more, until it feels like enough, and only then notice the success that was there for the taking. To change that thought habit requires a replacement thought, something like "I create success with ease instead of suffering." Anchoring that new thought can take some mental muscle, and that's where the visionbuilders' skill set comes in as your mental muscle builder.

Your Sneaky Comfort Zone

Your mindset can be devious. Your inner beliefs create your life, then hide and say, "No, it wasn't me; it was those guys out there!" Because it seems so clear that negative events come from outside forces, instead of from our own thoughts, it's logical to be wary of the unknown. So we create a way of being that feels safe. We limit our risks and keep life as small as our fears require. You may not be fulfilled, but at least you are safe from "those guys out there." This is your comfort zone.

Your comfort zone is a way of seeing the world and operating in it that feels safe, familiar, and comfortable. Everybody's got one;

it's part of your mindset. In your comfort zone, you reign over your life. Nothing threatens you; your power is secure. To stay there, you create a sort of safety suit. Like astronaut gear or a scuba tank, it provides an environment where you can breathe and feel protected, moving around with an umbilicus connecting you to safety. There may be crises and drama, but they are familiar; you have solved them before, and you can solve them again. Or, if you can't, at least the battleground is familiar.

The problem is, you can't build a vision wearing your safety suit, because everything you want is outside your comfort zone's borders. The nature of life is expansion, and expansion always means new experiences—the unknown.

Visionbuilding happens in the realm of the unknown. If you looked in a mirror while wearing your safety suit, what would you see? A safety suit! You wouldn't see the person inside it; you wouldn't know who you truly are. To build a vision, you must be visible to yourself, so you can know your hidden desires, strengths, weaknesses, and inner resources. The unknown "out there" beyond your comfort zone has to be visible too. By keeping you tethered to your known world, your safety suit prevents you from experiences that can help you build your dreams.

My e-mail signature line is *"Sometimes your only available transportation is a leap of faith."* It's the only way to transport you to your vision. You must go to the edge of your comfort zone, peel off your safety suit, put one foot into the unknown, and take at least a baby step into the abyss.

The Visionbuilders' Success Mindset

The best way to change beliefs is to replace them with better ones, intentionally planting them in your mind until they become part of your mindset. Struggling against what you want to change only makes the old beliefs stronger—but you already know that from experience.

The visionbuilders' success mindset is a set of beliefs that create the panoramic success that you desire and deserve. You want these beliefs to be the dominant mindset that generates your thoughts and actions.

The success mindset will support your highest business or personal vision. You'll learn how your conscious mind can plant the success mindset in your subconscious in Chapter 6. For now, think of the mindset as a group of positive affirmations; imagine that they are transforming any beliefs that hold you back into thoughts that build success. Soon you'll find that it's true.

The following is the visionbuilders' success mindset:

- It is my nature to create and contribute. It is why I am here.
- I am hardwired for panoramic success—free of struggle and suffering.
- Vision creates success that is easy, joyful, and fulfilling.
- Aware that life reflects beliefs, thoughts, and emotions; I choose my thoughts consciously, always pursuing vision.
- I am part of a universe of infinite potential, unconditional love, creativity, and intention. It is my source of insights, guidance, power, and freedom.
- I am powerful and valuable because of my universal nature.
- I develop self-mastery that establishes and maintains my success mindset.

Success Triangle Side Three: Whole-Brain Skill Set

I was in aerobics classes about five days a week, skilled enough that it shouldn't have happened. But one day in class I tripped over my own feet, fell on my butt, and tore a leg muscle. For the next six weeks, I hobbled around on crutches. I was working as a management consultant at the time—on and off lots of airplanes and standing to do presentations. I still remember how hard it was to function with only one leg. Everything took longer; it was frustrating, and there were some things I just couldn't do. It physically hampered my power.

If you're not your using your whole-brain intelligence, you hamper your power, too, not physically but mentally. You probably know that your brain has two sides or hemispheres. Brain scan studies have taught us what each side controls. The left side controls logical, linear, analytical thinking, and the right side controls creativity, insight, intuition, and big-picture thinking. There is a huge nerve bundle connecting them, which means you can use both at once.

Modern western societies overvalue left brain intelligence, probably because our analytical abilities distinguish us from lower animals (so we are told). Left-brain jobs pay premium salaries, whereas the "starving artist" is a classic modern reality. The second-class status of the right-brain means that most of us ignore or downplay our intuitive abilities. There's a problem with that; operating with only one side of your brain on the job is like hobbling around on crutches. You're missing half your power.

Intuition vs. Logic

Have your left-brain logic and right-brain intuition ever been at war with each other? If you're like most of us, logic won. Then soon you were slapping your forehead and saying, "*!#!, I knew I should have listened to my gut, followed my intuition, and trusted my instincts!" Science now supports what successful visionbuilders have always known—intuition is accurate, trustworthy, and wise.

Useful as it is, logic can be blind to invisible possibilities and unlimited potential. Logic is linear; it can't see around corners. It is clueless about the available wisdom of the universe. But your intuitive mind is fluid and open. It sees around corners, through walls, across space and time. You can trust intuition to light a path that logic can't.

My e-mail signature phrase, "Sometimes your only available transportation is a leap of faith," came to me in meditation (where intuition lives) and has helped me move forward ever since. In visionbuilding, it's easy to get scared and stuck, and your logic can keep you there, spinning in pros and cons. I've found that often my only way forward is to listen to intuition's voice, close my eyes, hold my breath, and then leap! Haven't had a crash landing yet.

Your intuition is not messages from outside yourself, or from your inner fears and ego. It is that still small voice that is always correct when you follow it and always correct in retrospect when you don't. Maybe you think of it as your gut instincts. The more you operate from that flawless inner voice and learn to ignore outside influences, the better is your chance of creating success. Your inner wisdom knows exactly how to get you there.

Recently, a client was afraid to take the advice of friends and colleagues about a big decision. He was concerned that they might have personal agendas, even subconscious ones, influencing their advice. The poor guy was really stuck, with no way to know if his suspicions were right or unfounded, because there's no true way to know another's motives. He really wanted their help, but could he trust it? My advice to him was "Don't. Ask and listen, be grateful and gracious, but don't trust what you hear." What! Isn't that paranoid and hardhearted? No. It isn't about not trusting others; instead, it's about trusting your own intuitive guidance.

We reviewed the visionbuilders' success triangle and intuition as part of whole-brain intelligence. When I explained to my client what intuition does, he wanted some. Intuition shows you what to trust in your world at the moment. You never have to worry about whether to trust other's motives, promises, or commitments, or even your own logic (which definitely is not foolproof). Instead you trust that inner voice that always leads you to your highest good.

Intuition was a great cure for the business paranoia that was torturing my client. It brought him peace and confidence, as well as the right decision he was after. Smart visionbuilders learn to unhook their attention from trying to figure out life's questions and partner up with their inner wisdom instead.

Your Built-In GPS

Relying on intuition is like having a personal inner GPS. My car's GPS (her name is Georgette) knows, via satellite, where I am in space at any moment. From that point, if I tell her where I want to go, she figures out the best route and gets me there, turn by turn. She tells me if I have a freeway exit coming up in two miles and, if I mess up, says flatly, "Make your first legal U-turn." Georgette never criticizes me but just objectively guides me along the best path. As you build your vision, your intuition is your GPS. Your part is to know where you are now (that's what the self-observation worksheet in Chapter 11 is for) so that you can make corrections as needed.

Clues to Intuition

Sometimes it's easy to recognize intuition. You experience a hunch or an "aha" moment that's unmistakable. Or maybe you see a symbolic image or have a dream that wakes you up with a powerful insight. Sometimes clues come as synchronicity—events that are so uncanny that they can't possibly be explained as coincidence. Joseph Jaworsky, in his book *Synchronicity*, tells his personal tale of following a vision through one synchronous event after another. The more he surrendered to his intuitive guidance, the more the universe seemed to orchestrate his success. For example, there was a man he desperately wanted to meet to get his ideas about a project, but every attempt failed. One day heading through the door of a hotel into the rain, a stranger handed him his umbrella. "Take this. I don't need it the rest of the day. You can leave it at the desk when you return." Jaworsky thanked him and asked his name. Can you guess who it was? The very man he had been so unsuccessfully trying to meet.

Emotions and physical sensations provide intuition clues too, although most people aren't as tuned in to them as they are to hunches or "aha's." Doesn't it make sense that, because your mind and body and emotions are all part of you, your intuition can grab your attention through physical and emotional cues?

I want to be clear that intuition is not an emotion, any more than logic is. It's a mental faculty, an innate discernment system that sends you "heads-up" signals. Emotional sensations that are positive and feel good are such signals, and sometimes negative emotions can be intuition's signals too. In both cases, there might be a feeling of relief or a reduction of stress. I remember when my proposal was being considered by the publishers of this book, I had an intuition that they were going to say yes, and it felt euphoric. I also remember a literary agent I talked to who gave me a "bad vibe." That "vibe" was clearly my intuition at work saying, "This is not the agent for you." Certain physical sensations can signal intuition too. A surge or drop in your energy, a feeling of tightness or tingling, a nervousness or anxiety can mean your intuition is at work.

The visionbuilders' self-observation worksheet that you'll work with later will give you some practice tuning in to intuition's specific signals. The following test is a tool for deciding when those signals are in play.

IS IT INTUITION OR INDIGESTION?

Seven questions that help you tell the difference.

A QUICK INTUITION TEST:
"Yes" answers indicate intuition is at work.

1. Did it come to me as an "Aha!" instead of a result of conscious mental labors?

2. Where do I feel the guidance as energy in my body? Head? Heart? Gut?

3. Does it stimulate my creativity, leading me to new ideas, insights?

4. Do I "sense" that the source of this guidance is beyond my human mind?

5. Does it lead me to a positive result?

6. Do I feel strong emotions that lead me to a decision?

7. Do I feel unburdened, relieved, at ease?

Bill's Gut

Bill had to make one of the toughest decisions of his life, whether or not to leave his business partnership of decades to pursue a dream. He did what many do; he asked his friends, family, and colleagues for advice. He also analyzed the option's pros and cons. Devoted to logic, he thought it all through. But he still couldn't decide. By the time he showed up at the visionbuilders' seminar, he had driven himself nearly nuts.

"OK, Bill," I said, "let's try this. Imagine putting everything everyone has told you, every shred of advice, into a big pile. Now sweep that pile out the door of your mind. Turn your focus into the deeper parts of your mind, think of it as your gut instincts if you want. It's just you and your inner guidance now, nobody else. Ask yourself the simple question you have been asking others—What should I do?" We sat together in the stillness until the "aha!" moment arrived.

I think Bill will never be the same. He learned that his intuition can be counted on for the truth—flawless, reliable truth, clear as a bell—about any circumstance. I knew Bill would make a success of his new business, because he had the confidence and courage that comes from knowing your whole-brain intelligence is at work—including intuition.

Intuition and Success

When I teach visionbuilders' skills to Type A personality, left-brain-oriented business folks and we get to intuition, some look at me like I'm a new-age nutcase. Even if I convince them that intuition is crucial to success, many are clueless about how to find it. What was that address again?

The logic and intuition of successful leaders are in good working order. They have the right cognitive, organizational skills, and well-developed intuitive abilities. Leaders commonly focus on control of processes and systems and on drawing logical conclusions from data. The most successful leaders use both left and right brain abilities to make good decisions. They have a competitive advantage that goes beyond decision making; they're good people managers, negotiators, and visionaries, who can dream the big dreams and have the discipline and structure to make them real.

Jonas Salk, respected creator of the polio vaccine, wrote, "The intuitive mind tells the logical mind where to look next." Richard Branson, creator of Virgin Atlantic airlines and Virgin Records, said, "I rely far more on gut instincts than on researching huge amounts of statistics." Warren Benis, best-selling author and business consultant, says listening to his "inner voice" is one of the best leadership lessons he ever learned.

There's lots of evidence that bringing the right side of the brain into the success-building game is the future. Books such as Malcolm Gladwell's *Blink*, James Surowiecki's *The Wisdom of Crowds*, and Daniel H. Pink's *A Whole New Mind: Why Right-Brainers Will Rule the Future* have helped bring these concepts into the business and personal mainstream. They describe the practical power of the individual and collective intuition and legitimize it as an innate sixth sense, with applications in all areas of life. *Trust Your Gut* by Richard Contino shows us how intuition trumps just about everything in the realm of business guidance. Malcolm Gladwell in *Blink* tells us about "thinking without thinking," about how we intuitively "know" from a place that is deeper and truer than logic. James Surowiecki in *The Wisdom of Crowds* offers exciting examples of how groups make better decisions than their smartest members. One of my favorites is a Princeton study that found crossword puzzles were solved six times faster by individuals after group meditation.

We began this section with how important it is to bring both sides of your brain onto the visionbuilding playing field. It's easy to understand that the left-brain part of the skill set is in fact a skill.

In school and in life in general, you learn to think logically, use your calculator, or fix the bathroom plumbing. It's all clearly skill development. But what about the right-brain faculties? Intuition, creativity, big-picture perception, pattern recognition—can these be learned like you learn to work your Smartphone? Yes. It's just a different process.

That process depends on the first of the nine visionbuilders' skills that support the success triangle. The skill of *stillness is* the foundation one and the one that enables you to develop your right-brain skills and to integrate both brain hemispheres. By stillness I don't mean silence, but finding that place in your mind that is absolutely still. There is no commotion there, just a quiet mind. You'll learn more about stillness in Chapter 6.

First, we have one more side of the success triangle to understand—self-mastery. As a segue from whole-brain intelligence to self-mastery, here is what Peter Senge has to say in his classic book, *The Fifth Discipline*: "People with high levels of personal mastery do not set out to integrate reason and intuition. Rather, they achieve it naturally as a by-product of their commitment to use all the resources at their disposal."

Success Triangle Side Three: Self-Mastery

When my son's National Guard unit was activated and deployed to Baghdad in 2004, I was frozen in fear. Adam was in his thirties and working as a mid-level manager for a large corporation. The Guard was about serving his country, sure, but the reality to that point had been fun one weekend a month with guys he'd gone to college with. I feared he wasn't adequately trained; I feared how the experience of war would change him. I feared he would be killed.

It wasn't going to help him if Mom was a basket case, so I knew I had a gargantuan self-mastery job. I couldn't change his circumstances, but I could change myself so I could support him and continue to function in my daily world. They say when a soldier goes to war, the family goes too. He was fighting insurgents; I was fighting my most harrowing fears.

For 10 months I did everything I knew to do, everything I taught in my visionbuilders work, everything I trusted. Ultimately, I asked myself, "If your worst fears happen, who do you want to be?" My answer, and the vision I cast for myself, was that I wanted to be a source of strength, courage, and peace for my remaining loved ones, and I wanted to continue giving my best to my work.

That was the vision in my mind when the call came. On patrol, their Humvee had been hit by an RPG (rocket-propelled grenade). One dead, three critically injured. Adam was airlifted to a hospital in Germany, where they sent those too severely wounded to make the trip home.

Only because I had diligently worked on self-mastery was I as strong and sane as I was—then and for the next three years as Adam recovered. Because my self-mastery includes the belief that I don't have to be perfect, I let myself draw inspiration and strength from him and from wherever else I found it, as I watched the slow restoration of his life. Surgery after surgery, physical and emotional pain, a Byzantine medical administration system, lost income, an uncertain future, Adam handled it all magnificently. The scars are no doubt deeper than what's visible on his surface, but I see that my mantra "All is well" is true. I owe a lot to self-mastery.

It's easy to see how the emotions of traumatic times make us lose our footing. We don't always realize that our subconscious beliefs and fears are always running the show. They don't always stop us in our tracks dramatically; it's often more insidious. We're only aware of a miniscule percentage of what's going on inside our heads, and our mindset is both filtering our perceptions and creating our experiences.

Self-mastery is mindset mastery, mastering fears, ego, old programming, and destructive habits of thought and action. It is taking control of how you react to what life dishes up. Self-mastery includes both mental and emotional mastery, using your mind to master your emotions.

The foundation principle of self-mastery is that everything dies from lack of attention. It's a well-established psychological truth that where you focus your attention expands and what you ignore diminishes. The strategy of ignoring unwanted behavior to extinguish it has been proven over and over. Parents tell their kids to ignore the schoolyard bully's taunts: "You're so skinny you could fit through a keyhole!" and "You're so fat you crack the sidewalk!" The taunts stop when they get no response. Bullies need partners to play their game; getting no response is a game ender.

Because of Failure School (Chapter 1), most of us have a bully living in our minds, taunting us with negative messages. Your messages are unique to your personal history, but everybody's inner bully expresses common basic themes: "You're not good enough" and "The world is a scary place." The good news for self-mastery seekers is that the same strategy that works for tormented third graders works for us. Feed what feeds your vision and starve what doesn't.

But how? It's mental muscle building—developing the mental chops to ignore thoughts that hold you back and focus on those that build success. The visionbuilders' skills help by giving you specific processes. When people tell me self-mastery seems impossible, I always give the same response: "Nobody but you lives inside your head." They usually say it helps. When you feel frustrated with the process—as you likely will when your ego and fears are vying for control—perhaps it will help you too. Tell yourself, "Nobody but me lives inside my head. I am in charge of my thoughts."

Maybe you've heard the saying "Change your thinking to change your life." Successful visionbuilders live by this immutable truth. If you're not convinced yet, think about how much effort you've put into skills that aren't about mindset mastery. It's a lot, isn't it? Yet here you are—wherever you are—still wanting something more and something different from life.

If you want your life or your business to change, you have to change, but change can be tough. If you've ever tried to lose weight, quit smoking, or let go of a grudge, you know firsthand just how tough. Changing who you are can feel threatening, so part of you will always want to hold onto the old you.

Self-mastery is not for the faint-hearted! It's a life-long process that requires sustained effort, commitment, humility, and lots of courage. Let's confront a reality together—nothing is free. Although the inner and outer changes that you must make are individual to you, what's universal is that your transformation into who you must become to live your vision has costs. It is a bargain, but it's not cheap. Remember, you have subconscious deep allegiances with ideas, beliefs, and relationships—that keep you stuck—that will have to change. What will you have to give up? Oh, let's see—relationships, security, comfort, values, your world and yourself as you know them. I wrote an article called "The Enemy of Great is Good," meaning that when we are comfortable or experiencing "good," it's hard to give that up, even for something really, really better, even something "great." The bald truth is that if you're not willing to lose in order to gain, you can't have your vision.

Ego, Fears, and Self-Mastery

The visionbuilders' definition of ego might be different than what you remember from your Psychology 101 class. For our purposes, ego means your unhealthy, irrational fears—both conscious and subconscious ones.

The ego's goal is to preserve itself by protecting the status quo of your life. There's nothing necessarily wrong with that, but, when your ego is running things, you can become your own victim. The ego's fears are up to no good. They lead you either in the direction of arrogance or in the direction of self-loathing. Neither is going to help you build your vision, and both are painful places to live.

Because you are both the owner and the primary victim of your ego, it can be hard to tell when it's running the show. But when you are working to manifest a vision, you can always tell whether the process is flowing or stuck. If it's stuck, you can bet your ego has gained control. Then it's time to get realigned with your vision.

We all have hidden fears that get activated with our desires to be, do, or have something better. Failed efforts at creating your best life mean that your hidden fears have gotten the upper hand. Visionbuilders learn to play tricks on their fears. An example is the affirmation "I am willing to change to have my best life." The phrase "I am willing" is less scary than "I am." It doesn't threaten your ego, or at least not as much, so you can move forward without its interference.

Notice that this affirmation doesn't lead to what your hidden fears are, where they came from, or whom to blame. It keeps your attention in the two places with the most power: (1) your inner growth and (2) your highest use. "I am willing" frees up qualities in you that your fears have denied and dreams that they have suppressed. You move into the fast lane, toward your highest potential.

A crossword puzzle clue gave me a great self-mastery lesson. The clue was "a petty or unimportant offense or fault," and the answer was the word "peccadillo." It made me wonder how life would be if I took all slights as peccadilloes. What if I went for the ultimate and just refused to ever be offended, no matter what? Life would indeed be different. The fears and negativity of my ego would be unemployed! To help myself in the process of banishing offense-taking, I developed this mantra: "It's just data, and data can't hurt me." It's worked so well that it's become part of the visionbuilders' litany.

Emotions Rule

This visionbuilders' principle can make all the difference. Emotions rule. It's the emotions behind your thoughts, words, or deeds that create your circumstances. The emotional nature of your thoughts overrides the objective content of your thoughts. You know intuitively when someone's words or actions and emotions don't match up. You know when your sister is angry with you even if smiles and she says she's not; and you react to that anger despite her words. Her emotions create your relationship in that moment. The dominant power of emotions is why self-mastery replaces thoughts that trigger negative emotions with thoughts that trigger positive feelings. You can't live a positive life from a negative mindset (vice versa, too). Visionbuilders work to manage their emotions above anything else because they know that's where their power is.

An entrepreneur I know has a subconscious fear of losing clients. The anxiety it causes makes him a poor negotiator, makes him underprice his services, and sometimes gets him stuck in decision making while opportunities slip away. If he weren't so self-aware, he would think his justifications for his circumstances were real. Instead he knows they are just that, justifications he makes up because he is subconsciously afraid. So he practices self-mastery, working to replace those fears with beliefs that support success. You are never at your best when your emotions are in charge. You are not your most powerful, and you suffer.

In the visionbuilders' program, we make a distinction between emotions and feelings. It may seem picky, but it's valuable because it can help you understand your responses to life, and that's crucial to building success. It's been said that there are only two sources of our behavior – fear and love. Emotions come from the ego and are rooted in fear. Emotions include anger, jealousy, frustration, shyness, hostility, surface happiness, despair, infatuation, and "cheap thrills." Feelings come from the heart and are rooted in love. Feelings include compassion, generosity, inclusiveness, fulfillment, peacefulness, acceptance, unconditional love, sadness, and joy. When you master your emotions, you free up the genuine feelings that better serve you and your vision.

Here is the principle. Positive energy, a positive frame of mind, sometimes called a positive thought atmosphere, creates positive experiences (and comes from authentic feelings described above). The same is true for negativity—a negative thought atmosphere creates negative experiences (and comes from fear and ego-based emotions described above). Emotions override everything. If you try to think a thought of success, but your thought energy is that of frustration or anger, that is the thought energy that gets perpetuated. More frustration and fear will be your next experience. Chapter 3 explains more about the creative power of thought and emotions. The visionbuilders' skills are designed to create the right thoughts and thought atmosphere to create success.

Reaching for Better Thoughts

Have you noticed how moods gather steam? A day begun in a funk only gets worse, and a day begun in good cheer keeps lifting your spirits—up and up, endorphins pumping and good feelings begetting more good feelings—until something causes a U-turn! You plummet downward, a miserable victim of circumstance. Most of us don't give much thought to how events control our moods, or even what our mood may be in any given moment.

Visionbuilders pay attention. They know that your emotional state creates your next moment. If you're about the business of visionbuilding, managing your emotional state is a crucial skill. How can you do that when events occur that cause you to react? You do it by putting you, not the circumstances, in charge. You, not outside events, become the cause of your mood. Emotional mastery skills help you soar to success.

This observation from Maya Angelou stopped me in my tracks: "Whining is not only graceless, but can be dangerous. It can alert a brute that a victim is in the neighborhood." Let that sink in for a minute. When a thought is a "whine," you guarantee yourself more of what you are complaining about. The negative thought, the complaint, will always stimulate negative emotions. Those negative emotions will create negative experiences, until self-mastery gains control.

A thought that defines you as a victim attracts to you more victim experiences. It attracts the neighborhood brutes, who will comply with your mental declaration that you are a victim. It's like wearing a sign on your forehead: "Victim here—all abusers welcome."

Changing neighborhoods doesn't help. The old saying "Wherever you go, there you are" is always in force. The only way to get rid of that sign it is to replace those thoughts with better ones—and fast. Every instant that you wallow and linger and analyze and complain creates more of the same.

What Are You Holding in Place?

When you've had a bad experience or thought about yourself or someone else and you keep thinking about it, you are holding it in place. As long as you feed it energy, it stays alive as a present experience, right there front and center in your mind—so you have that bad experience again and again. It repeats and repeats, re-stimulating its emotions. On the plus side, this is why we love to relive our happy experiences, to feel those endorphins surge again. On the minus side, it's why we continue to feel bad over perceived wounds and slights. That's a big minus.

Remember the previously described principles. Only when you stop feeding a negative thought can it become a past experience. The "holding in place" habit is usually unconscious, so the old scene sneaks up on you. Now you're stuck in old pain instead of building your vision.

There's a way to redirect your energy away from the negativity: a positive distraction. What's the first thing to do with crying infants? Dangle your keys in front of them or maybe a colorful toy. You might pick them up and bounce them. Why? To distract them. You instinctively know that if you can move children's attention to something fun, they'll likely stop crying. By moving their attention, you change their world. The upset is forgotten, and they are happily in a new experience. Cancer patients report miraculous healing by watching comedies nonstop. Pet therapy works wonders in hospitals and nursing homes. These are demonstrations of the power of positive distraction. It is one of your most valuable self-mastery tools.

Understanding the nature of your ego, mindset, emotions, the power of positive distraction, and the tough-mindedness needed for self-mastery are your foundation for working with the self-mastery keys that follow. Remember the basics. Your mindset contains subconscious beliefs that keep you from your vision. Change is both difficult and essential to living your dreams. Change stimulates fears and negative emotions, so you naturally resist it. With the right mental tools, you can replace those troublemaker beliefs with ones that create success. The key ideas and some of those tools are the following.

Seven Keys to Self-Mastery

You were born hardwired for success, tuned in to your flawless inner guidance, fearless, and believing in yourself. Self-mastery is your path back to that natural state. You can't become the magnificent being you are destined to be and live your destined magnificent life without it. These seven keys can help get you there.

7 KEYS
TO SELF MASTERY

1. **Self-awareness**

2. **"Seeing" your blind spots**

3. **WD-40© Power Questions**

4. **Self-love instead of Self-management**

5. **Comfortable Discomfort**

6. **A Happy Brain**

7. **Manage what stimulates your mind.**

1. Self-Awareness

Self-awareness is important, because the more you learn about yourself, the greater are your chances of self-mastery. The operant word in self-mastery is *self*. That means it is your own mind that you master, not someone else's behavior. Practicing self-mastery, if someone does something you don't like, you don't try to change them. You don't criticize or tell them the lengthy details of the distress they have caused. You don't analyze why they did what they did or negotiate for different behavior next time. Instead you understand that your distress is not about them, but about you.

Life is a mirror. (See the law of mindset mirroring in Chapter 2.) What I judge in you is actually something in myself that I need to look at and probably change. I am subconsciously giving myself a heads-up so I can improve me, not you, because I am the only person I can change. When you look at your judgments as a mirror, you see that they are a way to get your own attention so you can grow. What do you criticize in others and in the circumstances of your life? That's your mirror, showing you aspects of yourself that you need to heal, diminish, or develop.

Once you see what's in that virtual mirror, you can change what you know isn't serving you and your vision. You might notice that you've got a "struggle and suffer pattern" going on. You'll realize that there are people who succeed with joy instead of suffering, so you know it's possible. You'll decide to change your mind about success requiring suffering and observe yourself from then on. When you notice the old pattern, you'll quickly remind yourself, "This is just my old pattern; it is not the truth of my life. Success is easy and joyful." (This is an example of a good affirmation.)

2. Seeing Your Blind Spots

When you drive your car, that space behind you that is not in your line of vision is called the blind spot. We have blind spots, too, in our perception of life. We have limited peripheral vision, and we can't see around corners. There is always more to the story than we know—more than what we see in our moment of emotional reaction.

Have you had the experience of reacting to partial information and then regretting your reaction once you got the whole story? A client once went into a tailspin because she thought her husband had forgotten her birthday. Later that day, a florist delivered a gorgeous bouquet to her office, apologizing for the delay because of trouble finding the address and getting past building's security setup. Oops—all that energy wasted being upset about nothing. She had a blind spot that prevented her from seeing that her birthday was remembered, just not in the timing she expected.

The best way to see your blind spots is to first take a long slow breath. When you feel yourself in an emotional reaction, ready to jump to the worst conclusion, stop and just breathe. Let your blood pressure stabilize, still your mind, and then tell yourself this: "There is more to this than I can see. I calmly wait for the truth to unfold." What is in the blind spot space behind your car is revealed if you wait a few seconds, because that few seconds moves you to where the view is clearer. It's the same in life. Time moves you to where the view is clearer, away from your blind spots. But you still have to look, and that's where you need self-mastery.

3: The WD-40® Power Questions

I developed the questions a number of years ago, and some students say that they still hear my voice haunting them with them. (They don't always say this kindly!) The time to use the power questions is when life isn't going to your liking, when you're not manifesting your dreams, and especially when somebody is pushing your buttons. When you feel those reactions welling up, take a breath, and go to this question: "What more is there for me to see? To be? Or to set free?" You are asking yourself what you are not seeing because of your blind spots; what more must you become—more patient, compassionate, focused, courageous—whatever the situation is calling for; and what must you set free—prejudices, anger, suspicion, or small-mindedness. (Chapter 6 has more on the WD-40® questions.)

Here's an example. I settled into my window seat on the plane, smiled at the passenger taking the aisle seat, and felt a twinge of joy as the cabin door closed and the seat between us remained vacant. Don't you love it when the middle seat stays vacant? I didn't notice the cabin door reopening to admit one more passenger until the enormous unkempt man lumbered toward us and wedged his sweaty, smelly bulk into our vacant middle seat. He claimed both armrests and stuck one foot and leg into my foot space area. Did I mention this was a five-hour flight?

After about a half hour of simmering in righteous indignation, it was time for a talk with myself. "OK, Margaret Jean, time to choose. Do you want to continue to give this person power over your peace of mind? This little personal drama matters. You don't have to like him or this circumstance; you just have to choose peace." I wish I could impress you by saying my self-mastery is so evolved that it was easy. I had to do a prayer, a meditation, some deep breathing—and the WD-40® question! I learned that the whiny, judgmental, insensitive, self-righteous person sitting in my seat (that would be me) wanted to change. I took control of my emotions and decided who I wanted to be instead—peaceful, compassionate, and neutral to this man's physical presence.

The remaining four hours were a thoroughly different experience. Did he move? No, but my thoughts and attitudes did. The self-mastery practice of the WD-40® questions won me something far greater than things going my way—another step forward in my evolution.

As on that day, often the visionbuilders' WD-40® questions reveal things about myself I'd rather not know or deal with. But then I get over it and get on with it, and life gets better. I think you'll find that too.

4. Self-Love Instead of Self-Management

This is an important distinction on the road to self-mastery. If you think about self-mastery in the wrong way, it can make you feel bad about yourself, and that's bad! It's not healthy to criticize yourself and to think that you need to control your behavior in order to fix yourself. It can be a form of emotional self-abuse, as mild to severe as you make it. Examples are making yourself go to the gym, or making yourself control your temper in traffic. These have a punitive essence. You've been bad, and now you must do penance. If self-mastery is punishment, why would a normal person want to do it? You can see how important it is to understand self-mastery in the right way.

Think of self-mastery as a way to take your talents farther, express more of your genius, and bring your dreams into reality. Think of it as an inside-out process of expressing more of your true self, not an outside-in punitive management of your behavior. Think of it as being inspired by a vision, rather than being motivated by wanting to avoid punishment.

Real self-mastery is a gentle process that comes from self-love— valuing yourself enough to give yourself kindness and compassion. When you are looking in the mirror of your life, learning about your blind spots, that's an opportunity to appreciate yourself for taking that look and for cultivating a better mindset. Self-mastery is one of the biggest challenges in life. Not only does it require constant vigilance (looking at parts of yourself you may not like) and a willingness to grow, it requires something else that can be really, really hard...

5. Comfortable Discomfort

Visionbuilding is one big invitation to self-mastery. If you don't learn to love the whole process, the comfortable and the uncomfortable, you might as well just sign up for a minimum wage job building someone else's vision. Successful visionbuilders learn to practice comfortable discomfort.

Most of us love the idea of creating a vision. We love the romance of it—thinking about it, planning it, imagining it. We are excited about the "finished product" that will be our creation, the success we've dreamed of. It's the part in the middle that gets us. We want the middle to feel as good as the beginning and the end. The trouble is that the process of visionbuilding doesn't always feel good. It can contain struggle, failures, boredom, scary quantum leaps and stagnant pauses, self-knowledge we'd rather not know, dark nights of the soul, emotional intensity, confusion, a sense of being overwhelmed, and more—that we'd prefer not to encounter.

To become a successful visionbuilder, you must learn to love the process. How do you go the distance from inspiration to creation without caving in when the going gets tough? The answer is that you learn to be comfortable in the uncomfortable. If you want your vision, you must proceed through discomfort.

For that, you need self-mastery chops—tough-minded, tenacious use of the visionbuilders' skills. The best 1940s jazz sax players were said to have "chops," meaning "lips," that were highly skilled. From there, chops came to mean gutsy skill or powerful expertise. And that's what you need to be comfortable in the uncomfortable—comfortable discomfort.

Let's be clear: this doesn't mean delayed gratification. That is about suffering—toughing it out for the desired prize. Comfortable discomfort means relaxing into challenges, not struggling against them, and not labeling them as suffering, but defining them as part of a chosen process. You accept that it is an uncomfortable process and direct your energy to the visionbuilders' skills. Even when you'd rather whine and give up, you tell yourself: "I am a powerful creator. Every resource I need is within and around me. I have the chops to create this vision. I am comfortable in the whole process."

Visionbuilding always means venturing out from your comfort zone, and that is a self-mastery muscle builder. In your comfort zone, you feel safe and in control, unchallenged; nothing is at risk. Your ego wants you to live there, and your vision demands that you leave. It's a great irony. In order to gain greater self-mastery, you must leave your comfort zone, which requires even greater self-mastery!

You don't want to suffer for self-mastery, and, unless you learn to practice comfortable discomfort, you will. You must simply decide to love the adventure, the joy of discovering yourself and your success. The deep end of the pool is where the fun is.

Kim had a big business presentation coming up, and she was scared. Lacking both confidence and courage, she let her fears gain control and her ego run the show. Instead of doing what she knew to do—still her mind, relax, maybe get some physical exercise to clear her energy and sharpen her faculties—she tried to memorize and rehearse her presentation. Talk about stress!

This was a pattern for her, retreating into the mental realm where she could intellectualize. That was her comfort zone, but a comfort zone is never really comfortable, only familiar. Kim struggled and suffered. By the time of her visionbuilders mastermind team meeting two days before the presentation, she was a wreck. She had let herself lose focus and veered off her path. Fearful subconscious thoughts took over, and she was in trouble.

Lucky for Kim, her team stopped her in her tracks, got her refocused, and helped her build a plan. It included physical exercise twice a day for the next two days, meditation morning and evening, visualization exercises to create a virtual reality of the perfect presentation, plus superior nutrition, extra rest, and watching a comedy movie the night before the presentation. How did it end? Kim stuck to her plan and aced the presentation. More important, the whole experience strengthened her self-mastery skills.

6. A Happy Brain: Managing Your Brain Chemistry

Your imagination is your best friend and your worst enemy. You use your imagination to think of all that can go wrong. You put yourself in a state of fear and worry and negative emotions. Why not use your imagination to think better thoughts and put yourself in a state of positive emotion instead? Wouldn't you rather live in joy?

Psychologist Nora Volkow studied the brain chemical dopamine as it relates to addictions and behavior change. Pleasurable experiences (yummy food, a favorite song, cocaine, exercise, a remembered good experience) create a dopamine surge in your brain, then form a memory link so that the next time you are anywhere near that experience you get a new dopamine surge—a craving that motivates you to say yes to the experience. That "yes" creates more dopamine and reinforces the addiction. Addictions are about seeking a happy brain.

Visionbuilders use the happy brain practice to break cycles of negativity. If you are holding a negative attitude about a person, circumstance, or event, you aren't powerful. Emotions are in charge, instead of your whole-brain intelligence. By changing the emotions in the cycle, you can triumph over the negativity and get back in control. Here's how it works. A person, circumstance, or event causes a negative emotion. Using your imagination, you replace that negative emotion by inserting a positive emotion. Now you are in a better position to see with your whole-brain intelligence instead of through emotional reactions. That enables you to make an enlightened choice about what actions to take.

How do you change your emotions? By using your imagination. Your mind can't tell the difference between a real or imagined event. You start by thinking of an imagined event or something from your own history that creates a happy brain response for you. Next, while holding onto the positive emotions, you think of X – the troubling person, circumstance, or event. The process attaches the new positive emotions to X. That sets in motion a new cycle of response. The next time that you think of X, the newly established positive emotion will be your response. (Or not. Do the process again until it works.) There's a real life example below. You'll see how Rosemarie used the process to fulfill her entrepreneurial dreams.

Remember, it's your emotions that power your life. When you notice that your emotions aren't lined up with your intentions, you can replace negative emotions with positive feelings. By imagining positive experiences, you replace the negative experiences in your mind. That changes your reaction—and your brain chemistry. You trick your brain into a dopamine surge that forms a habit and reinforces the positive addiction. So, the next time that you think the thought that made you feel bad, dopamine is triggered, because that thought now has a positive association. Now that thought makes you feel good instead of bad.

Are you willing to give it a try? Good for you. Think of a vision that you are trying to create but that's not happening. Or think of a person, circumstance, or event that causes you distress. Notice specifically how you feel. How does your body feel? What is your posture? Is your breathing shallow or full? Are you sweating? Nervous? Anxious? What are your emotions? Next, describe to yourself what you would prefer to feel instead of these emotions. Remember, you're not imagining the circumstances as being different—but rather your emotional reaction as different. Next, recall or imagine something—anything—to raise the level of your emotions. Think of something that makes you feel joyful. Now, turn your attention back to the person, circumstance, or event that caused your distress. Can you feel a difference? Keep practicing until you can think of this and yet feel joyful.

The practice is called the visionbuilders' "joy or nothing" practice, because, until you can get to positive feelings, you don't think or act. It's joy—or nothing. When you feel bad about something you want to feel good about, you stop and imagine an experience that makes you feel better. That raises the levels of your emotions and begins to build a positive addiction to what you want to feel good about.

Here is how joy or nothing worked in real life. Rosemarie hated her job for years and wanted to go into business for herself. Finally, she had both the courage and the cash to open her dream business. You'd think she'd be in bliss, right? But guess what— she hated her new business. Affirmations, prayers, meditation, nothing worked. You can probably guess that poor Rosemarie was stuck in the mindset of being miserable at work. She subconsciously associated work with misery. So that mindset of suffering at work played out even in her dream job.

For Rosemarie, the joy or nothing practice was magic! Every time she caught herself feeling bad about something at work, she stopped, thought about something joyful, and then returned to her thoughts about work in her new happier emotional state. Soon the process created a positive addiction, cranking up dopamine when she thought of work, and ultimately changed her mindset. In a matter of months, she found the joy she was seeking as an entrepreneur.

7. Managing What Stimulates Your Mind

Visionbuilding is as much about avoiding what derails your vision as it is about pursuing what promotes it. The human mind needs stimulation; it is a natural and healthy craving. Where we get into trouble is in not taking charge of the kind of stimulation that we allow to penetrate our heads. If you are not exposing yourself to what nourishes your vision, your mind will be available for whatever stimulation it finds. It's not very discriminating in that regard; it's promiscuous and easily seduced.

It takes effort to build a vision. It is easier, faster, and cheaper to be stimulated by drama, crises, insults, illness, or injuries—your own or those of others. If you want your ideal to take form, you have to be as loyal and committed to it as you would to your most important relationships. You have to protect it from threats, including those from yourself. That means if you are building a vision of a new career, you don't allow yourself to be stimulated by dramas in your current one. You wrest your attention away and plant it firmly in the vision you want to create, letting that be your stimulation instead. If you have a vision of a healthier body, don't be stimulated by your maladies, but move your mind to the positive stimulation of the vitality you seek. You always have a choice about what you allow to stimulate your mind. Will you study marketing principles for a business you want to create or sit around watching cops and robbers on TV? Will you discuss the next step in your self-improvement plan or will you gossip? You always have a choice.

Threats to Your Vision

Because of our natural fear of change, we are all experts at self-sabotage. Beware of it as you build your vision. It is subtle and devious, posing as real and logical circumstances that happen to you—not because of you. You'll think, "Certainly I'm not doing this to myself—no way!"

Here is a list of some of the self-created threats that I have noticed in myself and other visionbuilders. Things we actually do to ourselves and to our visions. Even just being aware of your natural self-sabotage tendency and the ways it shows up can help prevent you from destroying your vision. Are any of these familiar? The next time that you encounter them, ask yourself, "Does this serve my vision?" If not, thank goodness you have this book!

Self-Created Threats to Your Vision

- Distractions of all sorts—people, places, events, emotions, dramas.
- Good causes that require your immediate devotion.

- Co-dependence. You need to learn about this if you don't already, because most of us have some (check out CODA, Codependents Anonymous).
- Physical illness and injuries.
- Mental illness, emotional illness, depression.
- Confusion: "I can't decide; I don't know what to do."
- The needs of others must come first.
- The opinions, criticisms, judgments of others hold you back.
- Never-ending new information, leading to more confusion.
- Something, or someone, new and engaging and exciting.
- Boredom, or a need for mental, physical, or emotional stimulation.
- Analysis paralysis: "I'm stuck because I still need more information."

Relax your way to your vision.

"You will succeed best when you put the restless, anxious side of affairs out of mind, and allow the restful side to live in your thoughts," says Margaret Stowe in *Elbert Hubbard's Scrap Book*, 1923.

If I could give you just one piece of advice that would help you on your self-mastery journey and in all your visionbuilding efforts, it would be to relax. When I'm stressed because something's not going my way, I tell myself, "Relax. Nobody's dead, and if they are, they're having more fun than you are right now." My friend, hypnotherapist Lynda Malerstein once sent me this relaxation process, and it's so good that I've used it and shared it ever since. She gave me permission to include it as one of our self-mastery tools.

RELAX:

A GUIDE TO SELF-HYPNOSIS[2]

This is a simple and effective relaxation exercise that will help you enter a state of light hypnosis. The more you do it, the easier and more effective it becomes. Some people see pictures or colors. Others just feel their muscles relaxing and achieve a state of calm. However you do it, whatever you experience will be just right.

1. Choose a time when you can relax undisturbed for about 15 minutes. Turn off the phone and move away from your computer. E-mail or whatever else might disturb you can wait.

2. Find a comfortable place to sit or lie down. Be sure your hands and feet are uncrossed so the breath can flow easily through the body. Many people find that their body temperature lowers when they do this relaxation, so you might want to cover yourself with a light blanket.

3. Breathe in and out slowly and deeply as you focus on a spot above you. Let your eyes roll up.

4. With each breath, count backward from ten to one. On the even numbers, open your eyes; on the odd numbers, close them. You will find your eyes getting heavier and heavier as you inhale and exhale, open and close.

   Ten: Inhale, eyes open
   Nine: Exhale, close your eyes
   Eight: Inhale, open your eyes
   Seven: Exhale, let them close
   Six: Inhale, eyes open
   Five: Exhale, eyes closed
   Four: Inhale, eyes open but feeling heavier
   Three: Exhale, eyes closed
   Two: Inhale, eyes open
   One: Exhale, eyes closed

---

2   From Lynda Malerstein, Board Certified Hypnotherapist, *Power Journeys Hypnosis*, www.powerjourneys.com

5. Your eyes will probably feel very heavy now. Continue breathing slowly and naturally, in and out, as you focus your attention inward. Notice the feeling as each breath fills your lungs, and then the feeling as each breath is released from your lungs. Notice everything beginning to slow down.

6. With your eyes closed, mentally focus on a spot at the top of your head and imagine that the muscles of your scalp are relaxing, like knots untying or rubber bands releasing. All those muscles are becoming loose and limp and so very comfortable.

7. Relaxation moves down across your forehead, down your temples, and around the muscles of your eyes. Tell yourself that your eyelids have become so relaxed that you feel as if they are sealed shut, and if you tried to open them you would find them so relaxed that the harder you tried to open them, the more surely they would remain closed. And you know that it is OK for them to remain that way until the end of the relaxation exercise.

8. Continue slow, rhythmic breathing as you imagine relaxation flowing down your body like a soothing, warm shower. Relax the muscles in your shoulders, neck, back, and spine. With every inhalation, breathe in peace and tranquility. With each exhalation, breathe out tension and stress.

9. Allow the relaxation to spread down your body, all the way down to the tips of your toes. Notice how comfortable you feel.

10. Now relax your mind as you have relaxed your body. Imagine or become aware of the number 100. Begin counting backward, repeating the words "deeper relaxed" after each number, until your mind becomes so relaxed that you forget to count and just sit or lie there enjoying the feeling of peace for as long as you feel comfortable. Tell yourself that each and every

breath you take brings you deeper relaxed, each and every sound you hear brings you deeper relaxed, every physical sensation brings you deeper and deeper relaxed.

11. When you are ready to emerge from hypnosis, imagine yourself counting from one to five, each number making you more aware of the space around you, and each breath you take making you more alert. At the count of five, your eyes will open. Or you may just let yourself know that you are ready to return to full awareness and slowly bring your attention back to the room. As you emerge, notice how refreshed, alert, and calm you feel.

When you are in situations where you need instant relaxation, take a deep breath in through your nose, hold it for a few seconds, then exhale slowly through an open mouth. Do this at least three times. Do this *everywhere*—at home, at work, in the car. Oxygen is one of the world's most effective and most easily accessible tranquilizers.

Enjoy your feelings of peace.

Final Reminders about self-mastery

Remember that self-mastery is a non-negotiable requirement of success. It is about you—self-mastery—not mastery of any outside circumstance. Distressing situations are a mirror with secrets to reveal about your growth. Remember the WD-40® questions. Practice self-love, not self-management. Love the discomfort outside your comfort zone, because that's where your best life is.

Part III

Visionbuilders' Skills

Chapter 6

INTENTION SKILLS

VISIONBUILDERS PROCESS

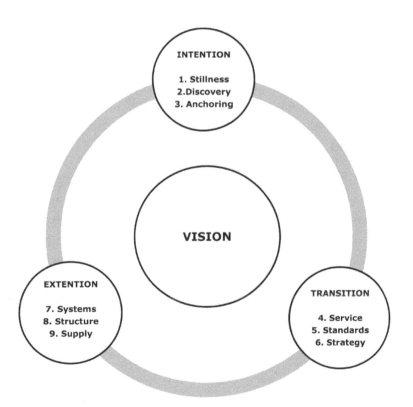

Your vision will become clear only when you look into your heart. Who looks outside, dreams. Who looks inside, awakens.

Carl Jung

L et's do a quick recap of what we know so far about the visionbuilding process. The visionbuilders' success triangle is your success blueprint or how-to model. At the center is vision, the engine that powers success. Vision is an imagined, ideal experience you want more than you fear change. The three triangle sides are self-mastery, command of thoughts, words, and deeds and making sure that actions match intentions; success mindset, establishing beliefs that consistently create success; and a whole-brain skill set that uses both brain hemispheres, combining logic and intuition to discover the right vision for right now and to bring it into form.

We're moving forward in your visionbuilders' skill development to that whole-brain skill set. The set of nine sequential skills support the visionbuilders' success triangle. They build vision in imagination first and then bring it into form. They manage thoughts and emotions so that your success mindset stays strong, and they establish structures and systems that make your vision real. They keep you grounded, focused, inspired, creative, and winning.

Intention skills are mental and intuitive skills that discover vision, lock it in your mind, and make change easy. The three intention skills are stillness, discovery, and anchoring. The stillness practice stills your mind, to perceive vision and inner guidance. Using stillness as a foundation, the discovery practice reveals vision, insights, clarity, and guidance for any life topic. Anchoring offers three aids that keep attention on the vision: affirmations, visualization, and physical anchors.

Skill One: Stillness

Stillness is the visionbuilders' foundation skill. It establishes the whole-brain intelligence that visionbuilders depend on. The stillness practice relaxes your mind and body so that your senses are at rest and your mind is clear. That state of mind makes you open to your right brain's natural intuition and your left brain's authentic logic. You are prepared to perceive insights, clarity, and guidance and to make the best decisions. With your whole-brain on the playing field, you are at your most powerful and most likely to win what, as a visionbuilder, you want most—your vision.

When I teach this skill, questions often come up about how stillness differs from meditation or prayer. Let's get clear on those distinctions. I created the stillness practice so that if you don't want to do meditation or prayer, you still have a way to access your inner wisdom and establish the mental discipline you need to build your vision.

There are studies that validate the many positive effects of meditation. There are well-documented physical and mental benefits; meditation is a respected path to spiritual growth. *Healing Words*, by Larry Dossey, MD, is a comprehensive evaluation of studies on the effects of prayer. (Interestingly, and supporting the visionbuilders' teaching, he found that the studies measuring the effects of "affirmative prayer" as opposed to prayers of petition- affirming vs. asking - most validated the power of prayer.)

However valid they have proven to be, meditation and prayer aren't going to help you in your visionbuilding if you don't believe in them and don't want to do them. But you need a way to still your mind and connect to your own inner wisdom and guidance. The stillness practice is a secular, simple process that gets you there.

A way to think of stillness is introspection or contemplation. Psychologists have shown that emotions are caused by underlying beliefs (what visionbuilders know as mindset). They commonly teach that changing problematic emotions requires understanding and analyzing them. Visionbuilders can succeed without delving into their psyches because of the power of a compelling vision to overpower negativity. Nonetheless, sometimes we get stuck and have to haul out the WD-40(R) question (see the following). When we do, we are employing introspection and contemplation, looking into our subconscious for an answer that will get us moving forward again.

The biggest challenge is quieting what Buddhists colorfully call the "monkey mind." Like a monkey swinging wildly from branch to branch, most of us have thoughts swinging around wildly in our heads, especially when we try to get still. I used to call my own attempts at meditation "fidgetation," because endless mental fidgeting was about all I could manage.

By adding the breathing practice that follows and removing the stress of an official meditation or prayer, the stillness skill becomes easier to master. It helps you relax your mind—which is the whole point. A relaxed mind is a mind open to insights and creative ideas. As you work with the stillness practice, tell yourself that you're developing mental discipline and a comfortable path to inner wisdom.

The Stillness Process

Rest quietly for a few minutes, seated, with your back supported and your eyes closed, letting your muscles relax, and easing away from mental stimulation. Any thoughts that have your attention now will be there later, so "park" them for now, setting them aside as you shift your focus to stillness.

Conscious breathing is next. It means paying attention to your breaths and to your body as you breathe. Most people breathe shallowly and high in the chest, a "fight or flight" habit learned from stress. Conscious breathing transforms stress into calm alertness and helps learning by oxygenating your brain. Eyes and mouth closed, relax your belly, then take a long low deep breath from its depths. Exhale through your nose, tightening your belly until your lungs feel completely emptied. Counting, slowly inhale hold for a beat, then exhale, 1-2-3-4-5-6-7. Do it three times, slowly and without stopping. This 1-2-3-4-5-6-7 pattern does two important things. It oxygenates your brain slowly so you don't get lightheaded. And the focus on counting and breathing calms your mind, taking your attention away from inner and outer distractions. As you return to breathing normally, stay relaxed, calm, and comfortable.

Next, imagine yourself feeling peace, comfort, and well-being. When you are fully in that experience, imagine that you have an awareness that goes beyond your human personality and senses, beyond what is stored in the data bank of your brain and the logical processes of your mind. That awareness is an innate natural ability that feels familiar and comfortable. Easy.

Now that you're in that infinite space, aware of your oneness with all life, it's time to set up your "channel selector" (or to use it if you've already set up your channels). Using your imagination, you create three locations in your mind. Think of them as radio or television channels or Internet sites, where you "tune in" to have a certain experience. You'll use your three channels for stillness and also for visionbuilders' practices such as vision discovery, anchoring, and standards.

The news channel: When you want insights, clarity, a vision, guidance, understanding, or awareness, tune in to this channel in your imagination. The vision discovery process uses this channel; so does the visionbuilders' WD-40® questions practice. The news channel is the channel that expands your perception.

The workout channel: Just as you go to the gym for a workout of your body, you go to this channel for a workout of your mind. It's where you do practices that require a disciplined mind, such as affirmations, visualizations, reframing, and managing emotions. The workout channel is the channel that changes your consciousness and builds your success mindset.

The peace channel: Sometimes you just get stuck. It happens to all of us, and we need a way to shift. Your ego and emotions have gotten the upper hand. Your mind gets stuck in "angry victim" or "judgment and criticism" mode, or maybe you're just agitated and need some calm. The peace channel is where you use your imagination to experience peace. It works like this: You recall or imagine a scene where you feel deep profound peace. In that scene, you know that all is well. You feel your connection to the universe and know that it always supports your well-being. The peace channel is the "reset" channel—where you reset your mind to peace.

The final step in the stillness skill is a repeat of the first two or three steps—deep relaxation, slow full breaths, and, if you wish, the breath counting process. Let your intuition tell you when you're ready to end the process. As you complete your stillness practice, set your intention to keep the inner stillness as your way of being.

Skill Two: Discovery

The visionbuilders' discovery process uses stillness as its foundation. From that state of mind, the discovery process reveals vision, insights, clarity, and guidance for any life topic. The process of vision discovery has its own separate chapter. Now, or when you're ready, go to Chapter 9, The Vision Discovery Process, for the step-by-step method and worksheets.

The discovery process is for more than vision discovery. Once you've moved into that state of stillness, you're in the perfect frame of mind for insights, clarity, and guidance about any topic that's got your attention or is troubling you. (The news channel is where you set your mental dial.) A few years ago, I created what's become the all-purpose questions for whatever might be ailing your visionbuilding: the visionbuilders WD-40® questions.

Visionbuilders WD-40® Questions

The next time that you're stuck in negativity and frustration, do something good for yourself and your vision. Get still (use the visionbuilders' stillness practice), breathe, and ask yourself the W-40® questions and the corollaries.

Just like the magical product, WD-40® that unsticks just about anything, these questions get you unstuck every time. I use them when somebody or something pushes my buttons, when I feel mistreated, misunderstood, or unappreciated, or when "they" didn't do "it" right—whatever "it" might be. I use them for the people and the circumstances that tick me off the most. The result of my use of these questions is that I need them less and less.

The WD-40® questions dissolve the enemy trio of anger, criticism, and self righteousness. They are your enemy because they harden your heart, close your mind, and disable your creativity. They render you powerless. When you're focused on anger, criticism, and self-righteousness, you are imprisoned by thoughts of what's wrong with the person or the circumstance, and you miss the larger understanding that can set you free.

"What more is there for me to see? To be? Or to set free?" These are the visionbuilders' WD-40® questions. Here's how they works. The questions move your attention from "them"—your perceived perpetrators—to you, the only place in which you have power (in case you hadn't noticed). Asking yourself "What more is there for me to see?" focuses you on yourself as the source of your distress. That helps you understand the wholeness of things, different viewpoints, and infinite creative possibilities.

"What more is there for me to be?" provides insight into your own part in creating what you want. You might realize that it would help to be more accepting, or compassionate or to communicate more clearly, or to listen more. Visionbuilders willing to become the person who can create their vision succeed, because they realize that the person they are now just recreates their status quo.

"What more is there for me to set free?" reveals what you need to let go. Beliefs, points of view, and attitudes that keep you from your vision have to be set aside. Maybe you want to be right? Maybe you've got some old ideas that need to change? Maybe you're too entrenched in your position? Maybe you're minding someone's business uninvited?

Corollary Questions

In your quest for self-mastery, the WD-40® questions are great power tools. These corollary questions supplement your efforts:

> *"Am I hired here?" (Is anyone paying me to sit in judgment of this person or circumstance?) I personally have never gotten a yes answer to this question, nor have any of my visionbuilders students.)*

> *"What is the highest use of my life right now?" or "What is my highest vision for this moment?" (If I died right this minute, am I doing what I want with my life?)*

> *"Whom do I chose to be in this moment?" (Do I want to be a victim, a perpetrator, a friend, a helper, a humble student of life—what?)*

> *"Where is my ego in this circumstance? (Oh-oh, I never like the answer to this one, but it always does me some good.)*

I have the visionbuilders' WD-40® questions made into bookmarks that I hand out at my seminars. People tell me the questions changed their lives. They say they hear my voice haunting them when they blame something or someone for their troubles. (They don't always say this kindly!)

Karen wanted to heal a relationship with her former husband. He abandoned her and her three young children more than 20 years ago. He contacted Karen last year, wanting to know his children and grandchildren and wanting to make peace with her. Karen had carried anger and resentment toward this man for decades.

It's hard to change that, but she was willing to try. She agreed to work with the visionbuilders' WD-40® power questions. Here's what she learned that helped her heal her partnership with her former husband and pave the way for family healing.

Asking "What more is there for me to see?" she saw that he was hurt and sad too and had suffered over the years. Realizing this helped her find compassion for him, and compassion is a path to healing. Asking "What more is there for me to be?" she learned she could be open to healing and open to the guidance of a higher power, and she could be willing to experience a better relationship with her former husband. Asking "What more is there for me to set free?" Karen learned that she had a belief that people don't change. She chose to let go of that belief and allow for the possibility that her ex-husband had changed and that the family relationship could change.

Karen asked another questions too. "What is the spiritual truth?" taught her that, within us all, is a desire for healthy loving partnerships and that love is stronger than fear. Asking "What is my highest vision for this moment?" she realized that she didn't want to hold onto the old acrimony anymore. She wanted peace with her former husband, and she wanted two parents in harmony with the family they had created. She wanted family gatherings that could include both parents comfortably, and she wanted her children to know their father as the person he is now. That was her vision. Karen's vision is not quite a living experience yet, but she is doing her part to make it real. She's happy with how things are progressing, and she is noticing how everyone involved seems to be participating in the vision in their own way, helping to make it happen.

Problem Reframing Practice

This practice uses stillness to refocus your thoughts away from problems and to create the experiences you want instead.

Putting your attention on problems makes them bigger, because you feed them with attention. The better way is to ignore them—that's right—and replace them with thoughts of the experiences you would prefer. Feed what you want, not what you don't want.

Start with the stillness practice. Tune your mental dial to the workout channel, because the problem reframing practice is a workout that builds mental muscle and a success mindset. Turn your attention to what you have defined as a problem right now in your life. Make a silent statement to yourself that describes it. Do your best to describe it as a current belief instead of a permanent truth. Take a deep breath. Now turn your statement around, reverse it, making it into a positive affirmation. For example, change "My boss never listens to me" to "My boss always listens to me" or "My boss is listening to me more each day" (if the first affirmation is too much of a stretch).

Next, create a visual image of what the affirmation would be like as an experience. Take another deep breath. Visualize each those statements—the problem and the positive affirmation—shaped like the word balloons that characters in the comics speak. Next, take all your energy and gather it together until you are about to burst. Now take a deep breath and let it out in one big burst of air—directing that burst of energy to the balloon that contains your affirmation—what you choose to be true. Notice that, as you do this, you are giving no attention to the other balloon where the problem is. You are creating what you want by giving it your strongest energy and ignoring what you don't want.

Skill Three: Anchoring:

Anchors keep boats and ships steady so they don't drift into dangerous waters or get tossed around in storms. The visionbuilders' skill of anchoring holds your vision steady so that your thoughts won't drift into the dangerous waters of fears and ego or get tossed around in stormy times. On your visionbuilders' journey, anchors keep you from losing your way and help you stay steady when you lose it anyway.

Whether your vision is personal, business, or a shared team effort, it's about creating something new. That always requires that you and your life change. Most of us have a love-hate relationship with change. We love the dream but hate the process. Change stimulates subconscious fears that make us want to run for cover. Insidious and devious, they make us lose our focus and our nerve. Fears are smart disguise artists; they know how to look like the most logical reasons in the world why you can't have what you want, or they show up as a case of the flu or a friend's crisis that you just have to attend to right this minute. Before you know it, self-sabotage has your vision in its grip. You're in dangerous waters. Time to zoom over to safer waters and drop anchor.

Anchoring is like a bookmark for your mind. It tags your vision so you can find it without having to start over when you lose your place. You create your clear, vivid, detailed vision in your mind; then you create triggers that remind you of that vision. Those triggers are your anchors.

Affirmations, visualizations, and physical objects are the best anchors, because together they stimulate all your senses and allow for differences in thinking styles. Our minds love stimulation and variety. By flooding your mind with different anchors, you increase your chances that your vision will always be front and center.

I interviewed the creator of a multimillion dollar company built from nothing but vision and hope. I asked him how he did it. His simple reply was "affirmations and visualization." He worked out on an exercise bike five days a week, and, during each workout, he would repeat affirmations about his business and then visualize orders rolling in. Those verbal and mental pictures anchored his vision. He added, "Every time I saw any kind of bicycle, I thought of my affirmations, and that would remind me to keep up my efforts." Without even trying, he had added bicycles as physical object anchors. Anchoring was a big part of how he grew his dream.

Anchors work in two ways:

1. They move your attention back to your vision, reminding you of it. That keeps you inspired and keeps dopamine and other happy brain chemicals pumping. A happy visionbuilder is a successful visionbuilder.
2. Because they keep your vision front and center in your mind, anchors stimulate you to take action—mental and physical—on behalf of your vision.

Let's do a quick overview of how affirmations and visualization work, in case you're not familiar with them or need a refresher. (There's more in Chapter 3.) Affirmations are short, positive, present-tense statements that you want to be true, such as "This business is growing and thriving" or "I always make great decisions." Keep your affirmations in the present tense. The universe precisely delivers the "order" placed by your intent; it doesn't read between the lines, so what you say is what you get. If you affirm in the future tense—"I will be successful soon"—that is precisely what you will experience—waiting for success in the future, instead of having it now.

It's important to remember that your mindset (powered by emotions) determines the success of your affirmations. If they are too much of a stretch, your subconscious mind will sabotage them in order to protect you. I used to believe that having lots of money would be a stressful and overwhelming responsibility. With that mindset, no matter how artfully I crafted affirmations or how faithfully I repeated them, my subconscious mind protected by not allowing me to make my affirmations real. I sabotaged myself by making losing investments and not following up on wealth-building opportunities. Only when I gave up those beliefs did my prosperity affirmations succeed.

Recent studies have shown that positive affirmations made subjects with measurably low self-esteem feel worse about themselves, not better. The explanation was that the affirmations highlighted their negative self-view. Right. It's like shining a spotlight on your muffin top waistline or receding hairline. You can't deny physical reality. It's too much of a stretch for your mind to accept.

But here's where it gets interesting. You can't deny what's in your belief system—your mindset. It's where your self-view lives and where emotions get stimulated. Positive affirmations and visualizations work just fine if you have the right mindset. But if your mindset beliefs and your affirmations don't line up, you'll be shining a spotlight on the contrast. And we know that what you focus on expands.

That's how affirmations and visualizations operate, and that's why the study went the way it did. Where you focus your attention expands in your experience. If you believe you're not very smart and you try affirming that you are a genius, your mind recognizes the contrast and replays that message "I'm not very smart." And that will make you feel bad.

With your affirmations and your perceived reality too far apart, you can't stretch enough to believe them, and fears sneak in and grab control again. The trick is to make the stretch just enough, but not too much. An example would be the difference between "I immediately change my mindset and my all my actions to fulfill my business vision" and "I am willing to make incremental changes to fulfill my business vision." The "willing" and "incremental" override fears. They provide enough of a stretch to be worthwhile, but not so much that your fears shut down the process.

Visualizations work the same as affirmations, but with mental pictures instead of words. Be sure that you visualize the complete experience, using all your senses, physical and environmental descriptions, and, especially, your joyful emotional state. Make a mental movie in which you are the star, joyfully living your vision. Here's an important point: if your visualization doesn't make you feel joyful, go back to the drawing board! (See the Vision Authenticity Test in Chapter 9.)

If you're not used to tools such as anchors, they can seem awkward or silly. Don't give up. They work, but you must be diligent—and watch that mindset. The average person has at least 75,000 thoughts daily. That means sustained attention is necessary to plant new thoughts in your subconscious mind. Anything less just doesn't cut it. Old beliefs dominate until they are transformed. The more you use anchors, the more you'll find your vision becoming real.

The use of physical object anchors has the same effect as affirmations and visualizations, plus one: They bring your vision into physical form. That makes it more real and strengthens your confidence. An author I know cut the phrase "best seller" from a newspaper and placed it on the photo of his own book cover. He framed it and hung it in his office so that he saw it every day. That physical anchor moved his mind to his vision every time he looked at it. It moved him away from negative thoughts lurking in his subconscious, ready to cause trouble. Mark Victor Hansen's book not only became a best seller, but it went on to spawn the famous series of "Chicken Soup for the Soul," co-authored by Jack Canfield and others.

Have fun finding or creating physical object anchors. Fill your home, car, workplace, and your mind with them. They will support your visionbuilding from the outside, just as your affirmations and visualizations support it from the inside.

When I was building the vision of my perfect mate and marriage, I first created the experience of that relationship in my mind, as clearly and vividly as I could, and then I created anchors. I had affirmations written all over my house and carried some with me. I visualized that ideal marriage, creating a scene of us at home cooking together for a family gathering, in love, peaceful, happy, lighthearted, fulfilled, and thriving in every way. I had lots of physical symbols of couples around me—candles in pairs, artwork depicting happy couples, and two places always set at my dining room table. There were times those anchors felt silly or obsessive, so I had to get over my resistance. It was all worth the effort, however, because I am now living in that vision. I have experienced the scene that I visualized and the affirmations that I wrote. After nearly a decade in my ideal marriage, I have personal proof. Anchors work.

Here's a final important point about anchoring. Work toward the best outcome you can imagine, and then leave room for the universe to deliver an even bigger and better result. Allow for a stretch beyond what seems possible. Unlimited possibilities are real, so always set your intention at the highest level you can. Every single person living his or her dreams is living the results of high intentions. High intentions are thoughts of the very best in human experience. They are based in love, never in fear. They are for something you value, not against something you think is wrong. They are about a positive vision, not about fixing anything broken in your world. High intentions are a deeper process than just setting positive goals. Intending to solve a problem seems like a high intention, but it is not, because the essence of problems is negative. A high intention creates a vision inspired by your highest ideals. It leaves a legacy of good.

Get busy creating anchors for your most heartfelt, exciting, highest vision. And remember this: The universe is always conspiring on your behalf. Your only challenge is to get out of your own way and accept it.

Chapter 7

TRANSITION SKILLS

Transition skills include standards, which describe, benchmark, and measure your success; strategy, which provides how-to implementation plans; and service, which means giving time, skills, and money to what supports your vision

The visionbuilders intention skills—stillness, discovery, and anchoring—are introspective processes. The extension skills are extroverted, experiential, action skills. Transition skills begin to move the vision from intention to experience. They are a bridge between the inner and outer.

These skills are important because they bridge the gap between what I believe are two kinds of visionbuilders. There are those who enjoy and are good at the vision discovery and those who enjoy and are good at the nuts-and-bolts implementation. Call it left-brain vs. right-brain, creative vs. rule followers, contemplative vs. action-oriented—we need it all to be successful. Whatever type you are, the transition skills will make it easier to work with the skills that aren't your strong suit.

Standards

When I made my living as a management consultant, the company I worked for had a saying, "If you can't measure it, you can't control it." It's not just an important truth for management consultants, but for visionbuilders too. There are practical and psychological reasons for standards that describe, benchmark, and measure your success.

Once you have defined your vision, it's natural to want to charge ahead into the actions that will turn that dream into real-time experience. But here is the big question: "How will you know when you're there?" Visionbuilding is a process, not an event. It takes sustained methodical effort, and it's easy to get lost in the daily chores. When you're swimming underwater, you need to stick your head up from time to time to see where the shore is and to mark your place. You have a defined standard—maybe getting to shore in 20 minutes—you have your goal in sight, and you know where you are in relation to it. You can proceed with your plan because you have progress markers and feedback on your efforts.

Standards make it easier to stay on track by defining what accomplishment looks like and by setting up progress markers. That's the practical benefit, and there's a psychological benefit too. I've seen more visionbuilders give up because of discouragement than because of external barriers. I myself once cancelled a new class I was testing because nobody had signed up two weeks before the start date. The very next day I got 13 e-mails from people wanting to take the class! I had become discouraged and given up too soon because I had not established a standard. With a standard—such as 6 people expressing interest by 2 weeks before the start date, at least 6 sign-ups one week before—I would have kept going, because I had objective progress markers. Without them, my emotions made my decision, a wrong one, both for me and those who lost the opportunity to take the class.

It's easy to set a standard with a vision that is tangible. If you have a vision of a healthier body, your standard might be that you can run five miles at 80% of your maximum heart rate, go a full year without getting sick, and ace your annual physical checkup. But can you set a standard for every vision?

Sometimes students tell me it's impossible to set a standard for their vision because it's too intangible or personal. I offer another truth from my management consulting days: "Everything is measurable." My favorite example is the story of a fellow in one of my Building Business Vision classes. Although Will thought he was there to create a new business, it turned out the vision he cared most about was to have a deeper spiritual experience. Developing a standard for a new business vision is easy. But building a vision of a deeper spiritual experience – how do you set a standard for that, let alone measure it? But we did. Will defined what elements make up a spiritual experience for him, such as feeling God's presence, feeling inwardly guided in his daily life, that sort of thing. Then he defined those measures for his ideal, on a 1–10 scale. For example, feeling God's presence to the fullest extent he could imagine would be a 10. The minimum feeling would be a 1. He rated what his experience was at the start, for each measure, and rated it again each consecutive week. It was awkward the first few weeks, but soon he loved it, for the reasons we love to measure things. It provided feedback so he could make course corrections, and it measured his progress so he could feel good about his efforts. Everything is measurable, and setting standards and measuring progress toward them is a great help to building your vision.

Strategy

Strategy provides the how-to implementation plans for meeting your vision's standards. Dictionaries define strategy as the art and science of devising and employing plans toward a goal. I love the art and science part—the notion that strategy is not just a product of left-brain logic, but also of creativity and intuition. If you develop your vision's strategy from a stillness practice, rather than trying to think it through, you've got your whole-brain intelligence at work. Both the art and science parts of your mind are stimulated, and that guarantees the best results.

Vision strategy is a step-by-step plan that fulfills your vision and touches each benchmark along the way. It's like a good hiking trail map that shows you where the trailhead is—your vision statement—and provides distance markers and points of interest—such as the footbridge is one-half mile from the waterfall. The map is a plan: you go from point A to B to C and onward until the end of the hike. In the same way, your strategy is an A-B-C plan. It maps out the actions that will get you from start to finish: your vision fulfilled.

But here's a caution: You don't want to be rigid about your strategy; flexibility lets you pause when something interesting shows up on the trail, such as that bull moose on one of our Wyoming hikes. He hung around, posing for his close-ups till he got bored and left to get on with his day. Flexibility lets you make course corrections too. If you come upon fallen rocks on the path, you might need to reroute. Your intuition will tell you when to press on with your strategy and when to figure out a course correction. There's no room for a "tough it out" attitude in visionbuilding. It should be fun and easy. If it's not, you need to adjust either your strategy or your attitude.

Strategy answers how-to questions. How will you bring your vision into form? What steps must you take? How will you get them done? What will you have to learn? Acquire? Change? Invest in? What support will you need? How will you get it? How will you be sure your benchmarks are met along the way? When you've answered these questions, your trail map should both make logical sense and feel right intuitively. So that's your final question: "Is this the right strategy?"

Let's return to the story about Will, the visionbuilder who wanted a deeper spiritual experience. His strategy challenge should make your own look easy. You'll remember he had created his standard and benchmark measurements, so we'll pick up from there. You'll see that they contain the seeds of strategy. Because he already decided to measure the quality of his spiritual experiences on the scale he devised, part of his strategy was those weekly assessments—a good start. Next, he had to ask the how-to questions. As he did, he determined that he'd need more opportunities to deepen his spiritual experiences, so he chose to expand his exposure to religious services—Buddhist, Catholic, New Thought, and Jewish. That was another strategy step. He further realized that he'd need to invest more time and effort in reading spiritual literature. He'd do online research and then buy the books or audio programs he wanted—another strategy step. From another question, he determined that he'd need some support, so he would look for a spiritually oriented mastermind team—yet another strategy step. Soon he had his full strategy in place. He checked it for rightness. Did the plan make sense? Did it feel right intuitively? Yes, he was good to go.

A final word about strategy and standards. Both can be valuable personal growth tools. They can strengthen your whole-brain intelligence, especially if you're heavily oriented in one direction at the expense of the other. Remember, one of the great gifts of visionbuilding is the personal development it stimulates. Ask yourself how you react to the prospect of developing standards and strategy for your vision and whether your reaction is stronger than neutral. Do you love it or hate it? Does it make you want to get started right now, or is resistance more your response? Your answers are clues to your thinking style and can help you use the standards and strategy skills as an opportunity to strengthen your whole-brain intelligence.

If you tend to be overly left-brain, you probably love planning and might have trouble being flexible. You'd do well to go lighter on strategy and heavier on flexibility. Make your strategy a general outline, with lots of room for inspired in-the-moment changes. As you work your plans, practice your intuition at every juncture, and think creatively about every challenge.

If you tend to be the creative, right-brain type to an extreme, you might balk at planning and measuring; it's not your thing. But strategy is your chance to develop those mental skills. You'd do well to spend time on a detailed plan and standards and then keep them front and center in your visionbuilding efforts. Be suspicious of your impulses to veer off the path, and be as disciplined with your strategy as you can manage.

Service

The service skill is asking yourself what specific service would best support your vision and then making a plan and a commitment. Service means giving your time, talents, and even money to what serves your vision.

You begin, of course, in stillness. It might lead you to do research or go out and observe some things in the world, but those actions come from stillness. Then, because it's a transition skill moving your vision from idea to reality, you move your plan into action.

Service isn't something you do just because you're a good person—although of course you are. You give service because it strengthens what strengthens your vision. Here are some examples. You have a vision of a healthier body, so you might volunteer at a health fair. You have a vision of your teenager being exposed to lots of career choices, so you set up a career day at his or her school. You have a vision of success as a restaurateur, so you write online testimonials for your favorite restaurants. You have a vision of a world free of poverty, so you donate money regularly to an antipoverty charity. Can you see how acts of service help build vision? What service might you do that would support what inspires your vision? Include it in your strategy and planning. Start small if it is foreign to your usual style, but make the commitment.

As you put your time, talents, and cash where your vision is, the practice of service serves you in other ways too. It reminds you of your oneness with all of life. It cultivates the quality of commitment. It establishes generosity and belief in your own prosperity in your mindset.

The most important guideline about the skill of service is to serve only from genuine heartfelt inspiration. Otherwise nobody wins. I make a distinction between being *in* service vs. being *of* service. Being in service means performing the functions that you have contracted to perform. You can be in service with a bad attitude and no inspiration, such as when you serve out of obligation or ego. Being of service brings sacredness to your efforts. It is not just a contract to perform certain functions, but a contract with your vision. You aren't just asking "What do I have to do to get what I want?" but "What can I do that serves this vision?" You are truly of service when your motivation is heartfelt and authentic.

If your life includes opportunities to participate in volunteer projects, decide whether you can truly be of service and then let that guide your yes or no. Check your inner guidance and ask, "Does this serve my vision and genuinely inspire me?" Please promise yourself you will never say yes out of obligation, because something is a good cause or just because it needs doing. Serve only from love and from what serves your vision. Then everybody wins—the service recipients, you, and your vision.

Chapter 8

EXTENSION SKILLS: SYSTEMS, STRUCTURE, AND SUPPLY

I ntention skills describe your vision and build it in your mind, transition skills move it from mental concept to plans, and extension skills are the nuts-and-bolts organization and resources that get you ready for action. They're called extension skills because they extend your vision, from an idea in your imagination to taking action in the world. As with the other skills, use the stillness practice as your foundation, so that you're employing whole-brain intelligence and getting the best from your efforts.

Extension skills are systems, which are specific measurable methods and processes that support strategy; structure, which involves order and organization that support systems; and supply, which includes tangible and intangible resources that fund your vision.

Systems

Systems are specific measurable methods or processes that get you to a specific goal. Dictionaries define a system as interacting, interrelated, or interdependent elements that form a whole. Systems are found in all of life. The human body is a system, and so are the economy, languages, your movie ticket purchase, and your favorite recipe. Scratch the surface of a successful business and you'll find good systems. The standard management roles of planning, directing, organizing measuring, and controlling are all about systems. Even harmonious households owe a lot to the systems its members follow: Thursday is trash day, so Wednesday night Junior rolls the cans to the curb; Saturday is shopping day, so Mom makes the list and consults with Dad, Junior, and Sis to be sure it's complete; Dad and Mom don't invite colleagues to dinner without clearing it with the other.

Conversely, when systems are missing, faulty, or there's insufficient compliance, you'll find chaos instead of harmony and failure instead of success. Systems make decisions a no-brainer, because the system you have established in advance makes the decision for you. Autopilot is making things easy: Who's taking out the trash tonight, buying the movie tickets, making the grocery list? It's not a decision or a concern because there's a system in place.

The visionbuilders skill of systems is the next logical step after strategy in successful visionbuilding. Systems support your strategy in a specific, ordered, goal-driven, and measurable way. Systems put processes in place that implement your plans. Your plan is the "what to do," and systems are how you'll get the "what" done. Don't overlook systems, even if you don't feel like taking the time to create them or don't believe they matter. They do. I guarantee you'll become a devoted systems thinker once you start working with them.

Let's look at an example. My husband and I hold a vision for apartment complexes that we own. Our vision statement is "All our tenants experience their highest ideal of home, and everyone involved with our properties thrives and prospers." The vision is an ideal of what we want the property to be and sometimes includes upgrading units to that standard. Our strategy is to upgrade a unit when a lease expires and a tenant moves. It's also to purchase materials (carpet, paint, cabinetry, tile) in bulk and to establish agreements with contractors for flat fees. The strategy helps keep downtime to a minimum—important because apartments under renovation aren't available for new tenants to enjoy and aren't generating revenue. What systems did we create to implement our strategy?

1. Renovation decision system: Our property manager notifies us of upcoming lease expirations, and then we decide whether to renovate or re-lease—a no-brainer decision, because we have established criteria (the visionbuilders' skill of Standards).

2. Contractor system: When we decide to renovate a unit, we notify our contractors, and they provide time and cost estimates. They do so in about 48 hours, because we gave them written parameters in advance. They've agreed in writing to a cost range for their labor, and we've agreed to use them for a certain number of renovations each year.

3. Materials system: Our property manager checks on what materials we have and what we might need to buy, lets us and contractors know, and shops for the best deals—because we've provided parameters and authority in advance.

4. Quality control system: We live out of state, so we visit the property just once a quarter. Twice a year, we go through every apartment and make notes on its condition and what needs attention. The manager sends us detailed digital photos of all work before we release payment. We can see whether cabinet doors are aligned right and be sure the carpets are the ones we authorized.

You can see how these systems implement our strategy and move us closer to making our vision real. They save us time, money, and stress, because most decisions are on autopilot. We rarely have crises and rarely have to do research or have long discussions about a next step. Systems do nearly all the work in advance, so autopilot can run the show.

It's your turn now. What systems will you need to implement your vision's strategy? Remember to start with the stillness skill, and remember to have fun expressing your natural creativity.

Structure

The visionbuilders' skill of structure is the organization that supports systems. It is the framework in which they operate. A business structure is a good example. Whether you're a small town ice-cream shop or a multinational manufacturer, your business needs the same basic systems—accounting, management, sales, and communications, right? So how do you get those systems into action? With a structure.

Your accounting system needs an accounting department, management systems need a structure of top and line managers, sales systems need field sales professionals and internal support, and communications systems need a technical setup of hardware, software, and technicians to keep things running. Then you need an overall structure to link the systems together. Here's what your management structure chart might look like.

A caution with this example is that traditional organization charts show hierarchical, top-down structures. The structure that you will put in place to implement your systems may be flat, circular, or linear. The format doesn't matter—as long as the structure links your systems together and makes them cohesively powerful.

Let's continue with the example of our vision for our investment properties. Our structure would be linear and look something like this:

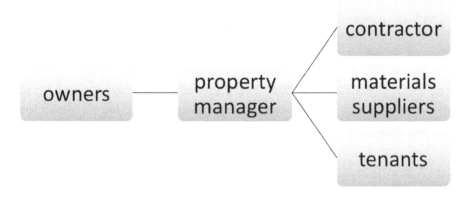

Sometimes people ask why systems come before structure in the order of our skills; shouldn't structure should come first? If you design the structure first, you risk hampering the system's potential, because the systems would need to fit into existing structure, and that can mean trouble. An example is a visionbuilders' client who wanted to add a new system for tracking customer satisfaction. He designed the system, described in writing how it could help the business and why it was cost-effective. His boss liked it – and rejected it. Why? Another department was responsible for customer relations. Any new system had to come through that department, not our client's department. This kind of frustration is common in the life of organizations. The more entrenched an existing structure is, the harder it can be to add or improve systems. In my years working with organizations on creating effective systems, I found that unless a system recommendation meant only a minor change in an existing structure, a structure change was necessary. As in our example above, that was often easier said than done. Whenever you have the opportunity to develop a system first, then the structure to support it, you'll be ahead in the game.

Let's consider one more example, Will, our visionbuilder wanting a more meaningful spiritual life. His strategy and systems included visiting various religious services, researching and working with spiritual books and audio programs, and finding a spiritually oriented mastermind team. What would be in his structure? It's his list of weekend religious services, his set of books and CDs, and his mastermind team schedule.

The question to ask yourself as you begin to set up your visionbuilding structure is this: "How will I structure my life or my business to support the strategy and systems that serve my vision?"

Supply

Dictionaries define supply as furnishing or providing. The skill of supply is about finding and applying tangible and intangible resources to build your vision. For a vision to exist in your world, instead of just in your head, it needs resources: people, opportunities, contacts, information, and money—because the things that money can buy will supply your vision.

I was able to spend three years in seminary, training for my vision of being a minister, because I had resources. My small business provided enough free time and adequate money. My spiritual community provided encouragement and mentors. I had access to the seminary classes and bookstores. I had a good computer and access to the Internet. If any one of those resources were missing, my dreams might have been sunk. For that reason, it's important to understand what resources you're going to need in advance. If you plan now how to acquire them, you can prevent shortage crises later.

So often people say they can't have their dreams because they don't have enough money. That can be a fear-induced excuse for not moving forward, but it can seem very real. I hope you understand that money is only one resource, not the one that matters most and not a reason to stall your dreams. If you believe money is a barrier to your vision, please go right now to Chapter 12, Self-Tests and learn about your money mindset. Doing what's necessary to have a healthy relationship with money will bless you in every area of life. And realize that dreams are built with much that is free—mentors, advice, opportunities, contacts, encouragement, library books, the Internet, free community programs, and the power of intention.

The reason this skill is called supply instead of money is that I want you to think first in terms of the various resources that you need and only later of how to get them. Money buys information, but that same information may be free. Conversely, some resources that we are used to having for free or functions that we are used to doing ourselves without hiring others might be a justifiable expense for your vision. Examples are the advice of a professional, a personal assistant, a bookkeeper, or a housekeeper.

Joe's story is primarily about supply, but also about structure and systems. I offer it at this juncture so that you can see the tie-ins among the three extension skills and also an example of what can happen to a vision without them.

Joe was working on his ideal retirement vision. His descriptions of what he wanted were clear and exciting. He was changing his mindset to support his vision. He had an idea of how much money he'd need and a strategy for saving and investing. It appeared that he was doing everything right, but the money wasn't happening.

At one of our visionbuilders' mastermind team meetings, I turned to Joe and asked, "So how much do you have now in the fund?" "What fund?" he replied. "Your retirement fund," I answered. "What retirement fund?" said Joe. Then it hit me—he has nowhere for the money to go! No account, no investment portfolio, no retirement piggy bank—nowhere! I got out an envelope, passed it around the room, and invited people to contribute their loose change or whatever they wanted. The amount collected wasn't the point. I labeled the envelope "Joe's Retirement Fund," handed it to him, and told him his assignment was to open a retirement account with the money—right away.

The new account provided what had been missing—a physical place for his retirement money to grow. The account prepared the outer world for what he was creating with his inner world. His vision was a dead end until he put to work the extension skills of structure, systems, and supply.

It's your turn now, for this final visionbuilders' skill. As you consider your vision and the eight steps you've completed so far, ask yourself—in stillness, of course—"What must I supply in order to bring my vision into reality?"

Chapter 9

VISION DISCOVERY PROCESS

Successful visionbuilding depends on accurately perceiving a vision—an originating inspiration or ideal imagined experience. The best way to perceive a vision is through whole-brain intelligence, putting both intuition and logic to work. In corporate America, the vision processes tend to be mostly logical, left-brain exercises. Native American vision quest ceremonies are intuitive, right-brain affairs. The visionbuilders' vision discovery process brings both ends of this spectrum together.

Neither mystical nor mechanical, it's a method that uses both intuition and logic to see into the larger awareness where vision lives. The process works for personal or business vision and individually or in groups. It starts with the stillness skill; then it adds questions designed to reveal a vision.

Vision Statement

The vision discovery process can bring forth lots of information, feelings, insights, and ideas. It's important to find, within all of that, a short summary vision statement that you can remember easily, tell others, display in physical form, and carry around with you. The other visionbuilders' skills help you stay focused on the vision and systematically bring it into form, but you have to start with a clear statement that has emotional power for you (and your team, if you're building a shared vision).

A good vision statement should be no more than 1–2 sentences, in present tense, and not about resources—"I want a billion dollars" is not a vision statement, but why you want it is one. It's about authentic creativity, and it should clearly benefit beyond one life. The statement should put you in the sensory experience of the vision and elicit positive feelings. Check your statement against the following vision authenticity test.

Here are some real-life examples of vision statements that meet our criteria.

Vision Statement Examples

"The Visionbuilders' Institute creates principled panoramic success for every life it touches by teaching original, proven methods for building business and personal vision."

"Our rental properties provide an ideal experience of home for all our tenants; every life connected to our properties thrives and prospers."

"The ABC cosmetic medical practice helps patients look good to feel good to do good."

"My vision is to write songs that inspire and teach the values I believe in, and that people say bring them joy."

The Vision Discovery Process: Part One

Stillness is the foundation of the visionbuilders' skill because it is the basis of the whole-brain approach to all the skills. The stillness practice relaxes mind and body so that the senses are at rest and the mind can open to its natural intuition and authentic logic.

Rest quietly for a few minutes, seated, back supported, eyes closed, letting muscles relax, and easing away from mental stimulation. Put away your concerns for now. Start with conscious breathing. Most people breathe shallowly and high in the chest, a habit learned from stress. Conscious breathing transforms stress into calm alertness and helps learning by oxygenating your brain. Eyes and mouth closed, relax your belly, and then take a long deep breath from its depths. Exhale though your nose, tightening your belly until your lungs feel completely emptied.

Count, slowly inhaling 1-2-3 and exhaling, 1-2-3, three times. Stop counting and just breathe deeply, staying relaxed and comfortable. Imagine yourself feeling peace, comfort, and well-being. Next imagine that you have awareness beyond your senses, beyond the data bank of your brain and the logic of your mind. That awareness is an innate natural ability that feels familiar and comfortable—easy.

Now, you or your team is ready to ask the vision discovery questions. If you're working alone, read through them and put several in your mind so you won't have to interrupt yourself. During the process, your whole-brain intelligence will reveal any other important ones. Working with a team, one person asks the questions, in a calm, even voice, leaving plenty of time in between. He or she will likely perceive answers too. The facilitator can collect and compile responses to distribute later but should invite sharing (of course, without permitting interruptions or criticism of results). Trust, relax, and enjoy. Work easy.

Vision Discovery Questions

- What is the authentic vision for _____ right now? (this business, family, organization, event, area of life, or whatever your topic)
- What is a vivid scene that describes it for my best understanding?

- What symbols can help me understand and create this vision?
- What words describe this vision as a vision statement?
- How can I best hold and develop this vision in my mind?
- What is my part in bringing this vision into form?
- Who else will help build this vision? What resources are needed?

Vision Legitimacy Test: Vetting the Vision

"How do I know it's real?" New visionbuilders often wonder how to be sure they have perceived the right vision. "How do I know it's real, authentic, legitimate, and not just something I made up?" It's an important question, because building a vision is an investment. You want the best assurance possible, just as if you were buying stocks, getting married, or picking your college major.

The vision legitimacy test is a criterion to help you tell the real deal from imposters. Only contenders that pass the test 100% are real, investment-worthy visions. The best way to take the test is to start with the visionbuilders' stillness skill, so that you are using both your intuitive and your logical mind. Whether you are a single entrepreneur—what some call a solo-preneur—a multinational corporation, or an individual looking for a vision in your personal life, the criterion is the same. Test your vision against these questions before you invest.

Vision Legitimacy Questions: How to Tell the Real Deal from Imposters

1) *Is it the prize, not just the process?*

   Sometimes individuals and organizations say their vision is to have more money or more customers. These are not visions. They are possible means to a vision, but they are not the vision itself. They are the process, not the prize. You have to look deeper. The question to ask is "So that . . . ?" In other words, you want more money so that something can happen, for example: "So I can learn to play the guitar." OK. The authentic vision is of you as a joyful skilled guitarist. Money is a means to that desired end. A company wants more customers—"So that . . . ?" The authentic vision might be about expanding into a new venture. More customers might bring revenue to fund that expansion, but they are not the vision. Be sure your eye is on the real prize. Is it a whole-brain guided vision, or just a brainstorm that resulted in a good idea? Did it derive from your individual and/or team intuition? Authentic whole-brain guidance is pure truth, free of undue influences. You recognize that truth through gut instinct intuition, a primal knowing deeper than logic.

Successful business leaders have said their gut leads them to the right logic, and whole-brain research tells us that's our source of the best decisions. Ask yourself whether the vision is a whole-brain guided one and then trust in it.

2) *How do I feel emotionally about this vision?*

I call this the "joy-meter" question. An authentic vision will make you feel positive emotionally (it feels right in your gut, too). Whether your vision is for an aspect of your personal life, your business, or your cause, an authentic vision will make you feel joyful. If it feels stressful, burdensome, or has any "should" energy about it—go back to square one. It's not the real deal. Even when they are struggling to overcome inner and outer challenges, visionbuilders don't suffer; the vision keeps them in a joyful emotional frame of mind.

3) *Does it benefit me and all who are part of it?*

An authentic vision benefits beyond just one life. It is the universe's way of benefiting both you and the world—kind of a leveraged blessing. A joyful skilled guitarist benefits the audience. An organization doing what it was born to do benefits its customers. An authentic vision is always selfish, in that it is personal (even for organizations), and at the same time, selfless, in that it benefits lives beyond its creators'.

4.   *Is it a stretch?*

An authentic vision is something to grow into, like a kid with a new bicycle he's not yet big enough to ride. Vision compels personal, professional, and organizational growth. I think it's the universe's devious way of stimulating our evolution—continual carrots just beyond arms' reach that keep us reaching. Do I/we have to learn something new? Is positive change required? Is it so grand it scares me? Can I do it alone or do I need help? Does it feel only barely possible? If the vision seems easy, small, and a no-brainer, it's probably not the real deal. Get back to work until you find the vision that feels like true love; it scares you silly, and you can't live without it.

5)   *Is it the right vision for right now?*

The old adage that there is a right time for everything is true for visions. Sometimes a vision can meet all the criteria described and yet not be right for this moment. If the vision is right but the timing is wrong, you will not succeed. Patience may be in order, or even focusing on another vision that is more appropriate for now. Sometimes visionbuilders want to start a business but hold on fiercely to secure salaried jobs. There may be mindset and financial stewardship work to do before starting an entrepreneurial vision. This final question makes sure that you don't get ahead of yourself. The right vision for right now keeps you succeeding and gaining skills for bigger and better visions as you progress. And remember, your answer is found in the stillness.

Visionbuilders' Worksheet

This is your planning sheet for building your vision. You'll work through the nine visionbuilders' skills in sequence. As you complete the various processes, log your results in this worksheet. When you've finished, you'll have a blueprint or roadmap to keep you focused and inspired. Because the visionbuilders' program is equally powerful for any area of life and because the skill gets better with practice, you can copy this worksheet to use again and again, for vision after vision. Or download a copy at www. visionbuildersinstitute.com

Vision Description

_____

_____

_____

_____

_____

_____

_____

Anchoring: Affirmations

_____

_____

_____

_____

_____

Visualization Description

_____

_____

_____

_____

_____

_____

_____

Physical Anchors

_____

_____

_____

_____

_____

_____

_____

Service Description(s)

_____

_____

_____

_____

_____

_____

_____

_____

Standards

_____

_____

_____

_____

_____

_____

Standards Benchmarks

_____

_____

_____

_____

_____

_____

_____

Strategy

_____

_____

_____

_____

_____

_____

_____

_____

Systems

_____

_____

_____

_____

_____

_____

_____

Structure

_____

_____

_____

_____

_____

_____

_____

_____

Supply

_____

_____

_____

_____

_____

_____

_____

_____

Chapter 10

BUILDING BUSINESS VISION

Special Tools for Entrepreneurs, Teams, and Organizations

"They're gone," she sobbed. "Every single one. I did exactly what you told me, and now six families, every customer I had—gone." She took a gulp of air, still crying. "Every single one. I can't believe this is happening!" Attention shifted to me, eyes around the table suspicious, expectant. "All of them? Wow. Perfect," I replied. "That's exactly what I hoped for."

Cathy was a new realtor, struggling to build her business. Following her broker's marketing program with precision and zeal, she'd attracted a steady stream of customers. The only problem was that they were "the customers from hell." She'd drive them all over town, buy them meals, stay up late doing research and crunching numbers. She exhausted herself trying to please. But the customers from hell were, well, hellish. They were belligerent, unreasonable, and manipulative; they lied and tried to cheat her. They didn't buy, or if they did, they'd buy from another realtor.

"Perfect," I repeated, "you had to lose those customers. You're doing great." The eyes around the table now turned from suspicious to hostile. How could I be so heartless! "Cathy, take a breath," I said. "Now, tell me why it is perfect that they are gone." She breathed and resettled herself in her chair. Cathy was a star student in my visionbuilders' class, and I knew she had the answer. "OK. I've created a clear vision of my ideal customers, and I'm practicing the visionbuilders' skills. That means the law of attraction is at work bringing the customers I want. But why can't I keep the ones I had? This feels so awful!" She was near tears again. "Wait, I get it!" another student interrupted. "I know what went wrong. She put her attention on her vision of her ideal customers, so there was no energy to sustain the bad ones! They had to disappear because they don't fit the vision. It's true; what happened is perfect!" Cathy's face relaxed, tears forgotten as she looked at me. "Cathy," I said, "you need to do only one thing. Keep your focus on your vision, and don't look back at what seems lost. What you saw as the bad in your life had to make room for the good. Trust yourself and the universe."

It took her a white-knuckled month, but new clients started showing up, the clients who fit her vision. They were enjoyable company. They respected her efforts and advice. They were ethical. They had the money to buy, and, even better—they bought from her! She loved being of service to her new clients. She thrived, and her business grew.

Cathy succeeded because she devotedly worked the visionbuilders' success triangle. She defined a clear compelling vision, developed a success mindset, practiced self-mastery and used whole-brain skills to bring her vision into form. How did that work? Whether you're an entrepreneur like Cathy, a small not-for-profit, or a multinational conglomerate, here is how building a vision creates lasting success:

VISION BUILDS
BUSINESS SUCCESS because it:

- Focuses resources

- Strengthens your brand

- Engages both minds and hearts

- Stimulates both personal
and organizational growth

- Makes the best decisions by
transcending politics and personalities

- Builds teams, collaborations and cooperation

- Illuminates the path to success

- Removes fears and resistance to change

Although visionbuilding is a powerful path to business success, that path can have lots of pitfalls. Problems with communications, politics, personalities, corporate culture, organizational structures, systems, resources, and outside influences can make the journey a tough one. Some of the most common detours, distractions, and de-motivators are listed here. Knowing what they are helps you plan visionbuilding strategies to prevent them.

DETOURS, DISTRACTIONS and DE-MOTIVATORS:

- Wrong vision – doesn't inspire, uplift, resonate.

- Fails to express the uniqueness of the business.

- Wrong influences or motives, politics, personalities

- Wrong mindset – doesn't support success, causes resistance to change.

- Structure and systems barriers.

- Corporate culture barriers.

- Flawed processes for discovering and/or growing the Vision.

With all these potential problems, how does an organization successfully build its vision? The tools and skills in the previous chapters are your foundation. If you skipped directly to this chapter, go back and read Chapters 5 through 9. Once you have that foundation, these ideas, tools, and tips will help with your individual business vision or your team or organization's shared vision.

First let's review two points that are true for any visionbuilder, whether it's one person or an organization of thousands.

1. Success is an inside job. External business conditions, the economy, the so-called competition, the political party in power, really, truly don't matter. Vision and the

success triangle of mindset, self-mastery, and whole-brain skills make or break success.

2. Organizations are collections of individuals joined by common purpose. They form an entity that behaves like its dominant leaders plus every individual personality. The visionbuilders' principles and skills apply to any entity, whether it's made of one person or a million.

"To Do's" for Shared Visionbuilding

In shared visionbuilding, there are considerations that individual visionbuilders can skip. Because you're dealing with an organization or team, all stakeholders—every individual who has a stake in the collective success—have to support the vision. And you want that support to be authentic, coming from their participation in the process and from genuine inspiration. You might think of the following considerations as critical success factors—things that have to go right for successful shared visionbuilding.

- Aligning organization culture and mindset with the vision
- Aligning structures, systems, processes, and resources with the vision
- Aligning unofficial and official leaders with the vision
- Shared definitions of success and progress measurement
- Shared anchor symbols of the vision (See Anchoring, Chapter 5)
- Group process participation of all stakeholders
- Self-mastery, personal and professional development of stakeholders

Shared Visionbuilding: The Whole-Brain Team

Visionbuilders are always compelled to achieve personal growth and to make the changes that a corporate vision demands; organization members must change personally. Everybody gets opportunities for increased maturity and new skills. All are invited to become someone who can live in the new vision. Leaders are asked to step up to a higher potential and then serve as role models and teachers.

But the unique magic of shared visionbuilding is the authentic cohesiveness and organizational development that it engenders. In a sense, the whole organization becomes a mastermind team— supporting members in their individual efforts for the collective vision. Shared visionbuilding is more than team building or motivating the troops. It is engaging individual hearts and minds as a unified force for the collective good—the vision.

Individuals working together create a collective mind greater than the sum of its parts. There's growing evidence of the power of collective intelligence, what I call the whole-team brain. In *The Wisdom of Crowds*, James Surowiecki shows that groups make better decisions than their smartest members. A fairgrounds crowd guessed an ox's weight within one pound, even though not a single individual guesser came close. Not convincing enough? Consider the stock market's response after the 1986 Challenger explosion. Of the four corporations supplying equipment to the project, all their stocks fell within an hour. That's not surprising, but, by the end of that day, three of the stocks dropped an average of 3%, whereas one dropped 12%. How to explain that big difference? The collective intelligence of the market somehow understood what an investigation would not reveal for six months: the O-ring seals on the booster rockets that caused the disaster were made by Morton Thiokol—the company whose stock plummeted 12%. Collective intelligence is real, and a great asset to shared visionbuilding.

Doesn't it make sense to put teams on the job of defining, directing, and developing your corporate vision? A church board of directors hired me to help them create a vision for their ideal new pastor and bring that vision into form. How did we succeed so well that, in less than a year, that pastor was happily on board and membership nearly doubled? The answer is visionbuilders' teams. Collective wisdom made it happen. Every step was done by a team, using the stillness practice do reveal the right vision, anchors, standards, strategies, the whole process. Each team was trained in the steps and agreed to this intention: To be open to revelations, insights, new possibilities, creative solutions found in stillness, and to personal growth in service to the vision.

Mindset

The visionbuilders' success mindset (Chapter 5) is the set of beliefs and attitudes that help guarantee success. But there are special mindset considerations in shared visionbuilding. For example, if you have a hidden belief that money is evil, how can you help expand profits? If you fear change, how can you support organizational growth? How can you learn new skills and new ways of being? If you crave power, how can you defer to collective wisdom? As an organization member, it's important to ask yourself, "What in my personal mindset needs to change in order to support the shared vision?

Organizations have a mindset too, a collective one as part of the organizational culture. Shared visionbuilding efforts will be filtered through that mindset, so it's helpful to define it consciously and consider carefully what it should include. The 2008 Obama presidential campaign had the mantra "low ego, low conflict." That mantra was a key part of its mindset. As time went on, the campaign became known for its exceptional order, organization, and attitude of respect. It's a great example of how mindset permeates an organization and drives its operations.

What's your organization's mindset? What should it contain to successfully build the corporate vision?

Re-Thinking Competition

A key element of any corporate mindset is how it views competition. It influences decisions about marketing, branding, spending, risk taking, and measuring success. Competition can be a prison in which you are both jailor and prisoner. It ties you to judgment and criticism of yourself and others. It ties you to concepts of failure and loss. It ties you to the past and the future, so you lose the power of now. Competition ties you to the opinions and standards of others, at the expense of your own wisdom.

Visionbuilders win without competing. They don't believe in it. They act from a different and more powerful point of view—one that expands their businesses, frees their creativity, makes work fun, and ensures their prosperity. Instead of competition, visionbuilders think in terms of completion—completion of steps and processes and, ultimately, of their vision. They spend their efforts on creating and offering their best unique products or service and trust that uniqueness to find its own success.

Visionbuilders know competition is not real. They have no competitors (and neither does anyone else), because they are selling uniqueness. You or your organization's vision has its own unique market, and no other product or service can meet that market's needs. Visionbuilders expand the pie. They understand that a larger market benefits everyone—you, your market partners, and all those eager customers. When you consider competitors as market partners who expand shared markets with excellence and integrity, everybody wins. Visionbuilders affirm: "I/we focus on creating my/our best products or services and allow the market to expand through shared success with my/our market partners."

Self-Mastery for Leaders

Visionaries . . . pull people up, spreading the seeds of positive vision so that it takes root in others and finds its way into our common reality.

Jamie Walters

Whether you're leading yourself to entrepreneurial success in your one-person enterprise or responsible for leading others in an organization, self-mastery can make or break leaders. You will find guidance in Chapter 5: The Visionbuilders Success Triangle, Self-Mastery. But there are special self-mastery considerations for leaders. And don't forget mastery of the powerful perspective on competition.

Corporate Ego Mastery

Self-mastery is ego mastery—controlling irrational subconscious fears. As collections of people, organizations develop a collective ego that acts just as yours or mine does. That corporate ego can cause bad decisions—from trying to protect its self-image—and can prevent the company from taking risks that are important to its success. Leaders need to understand their organization's ego and apply the same self-mastery tools they would for their own egos.

A Critical Tool for Critical Leaders

> *I always prefer to believe the best of everybody; it saves so much trouble.*
>
> Rudyard Kipling

When someone isn't doing his or her job well, it's common to judge and criticize. I might look at an unhelpful store clerk and think, "Geez, you either don't know what you're doing or you don't care." We've been taught that skills and motivation are key to how well people do their jobs. But poor skills and motivation often reflect a lack of good systems. The right systems develop skills and inspire motivation. I teach leaders to take a systems perspective in dealing with people.

Unlike human dynamics, systems are neutral. A system doesn't have a personality or hidden motives. The natural world operates on systems: it's how plants grow, creatures replicate themselves, and the sun rises and sets. In business, systems thinking means managing organizations by managing systems. I'm a big fan of this approach, because I've seen its results. When a business is functioning well, effective systems are in place. When it is not, it is a call for better systems. Systems is in the visionbuilders' skill set as a tool, and it's also a perspective or point of view that can make better leaders.

It can take some self-mastery, however, because we've been trained to blame the person. So when you are looking at poor performance, considering it as a system flaw doesn't feel natural. When you are about to criticize someone—stop and use systems thinking instead. Think at a level above appearances, beyond personalities and behavior, and realize that we all live in systems. Ask yourself, "What system is not working that needs improving? What new system needs to be created?" This not only diffuses your annoyance but engages the better part of you—your creativity. It's self-mastery practice that can make a big difference.

The ideas and tools in this chapter are for the broadest definition of "business." Use them not just for your for-profit enterprise but for community organizations, sports teams, family, church, political groups . . . anywhere you are part of offering a product or service. Think of them as knowledge and skills that make you a specialist. A general medical practitioner treats the whole person, just as your visionbuilding skills aid every area of life. A heart surgeon or psychiatrist treats a specific aspect of a person's life. As a business visionbuilder, you are a specialist too. You have better ways to offer better products or services, and you create business success that feeds both your bank account and your soul.

Chapter 11

BONUS POWER TOOLS

Before we were married, my husband once loaned me a power screwdriver to remove some cupboard doors in my condo, and I fell in love with power tools. "Real guys" already know this, but I didn't—power tools are miracles. They give you strength and precision and, well, power you don't have without them. They save time and effort, and you get consistently good results. Power tools rule! This chapter gives you power tools that make it easier and faster to build your vision. They are practical methods I've tried on myself and on both willing and unwilling students over the years! These power tools work—but, like anything, only to the extent that you work them. Give them a try—the ones that feel comfortable and especially the ones that don't!

The Visionbuilders' 49 Grateful Minutes Practice

Sometimes visionbuilding can feel stressful. The opposite of stress is calm, and calm is more than just a better feeling. When your mind is calm, your body systems function better, your brain chemistry is healthier, and you are more able to use the whole-brain intelligence that visionbuilders need—both logic and intuition.

Maybe you have favorite stress reducers, such as beer and pizza or a good primal scream. Here's an alternative, the visionbuilders' 49 grateful minutes practice. Gratitude is a great stress reducer, because it shifts your focus away from whatever creates the stress and toward thoughts that not only feel better but do you some good. The law of attraction is always in effect, so your gratitude creates more of the experiences for which you are grateful.

The 49 grateful minutes practice is simple. Seven minutes of gratitude a day for seven days equals 49 grateful minutes. Anytime during your day, get still for 7 minutes, take a few deep breaths, and relax. Focus your attention on gratitude. The special twist is that you focus on one of the seven areas of life each day, so that, by the end of the week, you have experienced gratitude for all of them. These are the seven areas with some examples of gratitude.

- Day one = gratitude for your physical body (How miraculously it functions, its strength, wellness, etc.)
- Day two = your emotional well-being (You're not crazy! You handle most of life pretty well.)
- Day three = your mental strength and intelligence (You have skills, abilities, knowledge, and you get smarter all the time.)
- Day four = your financial well-being (You have food and shelter and income; your basic needs are met and probably more.)
- Day five = your spiritual well-being, sense of peace, and connection to all life
- Day six = your relationships (Most of your relationships function well and are caring; those that are problematic can help you grow.)
- Day seven = your work and creative expression (You are useful and productive and give of your unique gifts to others.)

That's it. At the end of one week, you have experienced gratitude in every area of your life. You have set in motion more for which to be grateful, and you have had at least 49 minutes of calm, stress-free living. It's a good start.

The Seven Life Structures

When you pursue a vision for one area of your life, the results show up in every area of your life. For example, if you hold a vision of philanthropy and claim greater prosperity in the process, you'll find that the resulting greater income affects your physical being, your peace of mind, your creativity, your relationships, etc. If you hold a vision for healthier relationships in families, you have improved work relationships, which cause you to be more creative and fulfilled in your job, and you experience greater emotional peace of mind and greater prosperity. These are more than just side effects. They are because of the holistic nature of life. Your life is an integrated system, so a change in one aspect affects the whole.

Conversely, if you have a blind spot in one area of life, it leaves tracks in all areas. If you want to know where your blind spots are, just look at your life. Your blind spots have themes –tracks that run through all your life structures. For example, a blind spot having to do with supply might show up as financial lack, lack of creativity in your work life, lack of fulfilling relationships, lack of emotional joy, or lack of physical health. There will always be good, logical reasons and excuses for these lacks, and you may not always be able to connect the dots and see the theme. But it's there nonetheless.

Maybe you already understand of the power of your thoughts, the presence of universal love in your life, and the laws that tie it all together. Maybe you know that you are programmed to thrive, to be happy, productive, and at peace. Yet, perhaps your life doesn't always reflect what you know. The visionbuilders' seven structures of life is a tool to help you look at your life, piece by piece, so you can see the blind spots. Once seen, some will go away, just as a result of what researchers call "the spotlight effect"—awareness alone causes them to diminish; others will require some strategic effort.

A structure is a framework that holds something together or through which something flows. The building that houses your favorite fast-food joint is held together by its structure. A gasoline engine is a structure through which gasoline flows and is transformed into energy to run your car. You can see that the structure isn't the whole story of the building or the car, but it is a vantage point for observing the whole story. We're going to look at your life through seven structures. The point of dissecting life this way is that sometimes looking at the whole disguises important information about its parts, and you can only learn that information by considering the parts separately. If you show up at a hospital and say, "I hurt," the doctors will need to know more in order to help you. They'll ask you questions and perform fancy diagnostic tests to find out where you hurt, why, and what it means—before deciding what's next. Our process is a way of finding out more precisely where you hurt, why, and what it means, in order for you to help yourself create the life you want.

The exercises that follow are designed to help you change your beliefs, which are creating your unacceptable experiences. Notice the word *unacceptable*. It is a strong word. You won't be motivated to change by anything less. You must be at a point where you say, "This is no longer acceptable. I won't accept it any longer. I can and I will change it, no matter what." When you reach the point of saying that, you're ready to get results.

Read the seven structures of life and power tool exercises to help you build your vision throughout each life structure.

THE SEVEN LIFE STRUCTURES

1. Physical

2. Emotional

3. Mental

4. Spiritual

5. Supply

6. Relationships

7. Creativity/Work

The Seven Life Structures

Physical

In order to build your vision, you must attend to your physical being. It does not treat you well if you ignore it. Just like all the structures of life, your physical body is a manifestation of your consciousness. Most people realize that stress weakens your immune system; managing your stress with your conscious mind keeps you healthier. It's also true that increasing your stress with your subconscious mind will get you sick—sometimes big-time, life-threatening sick.

Your body offers great clues to what's in your mindset. Louise Hay has done landmark work on the subject, especially her classic book *You Can Heal Your Life*. It goes beyond describing the mind-body connection to show you how you can control your health by controlling your thoughts. Change happens in biological time, so your body will mark the change process. You can monitor your changing consciousness by monitoring your body.

Emotional

It is useful to divide this life structure into two categories, emotions and feelings. Emotions are the ego's reactions to events that are real or imagined. They are why you still don't speak to your aunt Tillie who told you your dog was ugly when you were 10 years old. They are also why you haven't realized your dreams. The powerful emotion of fear will run your life if you let it. It is a beast you have to ignore in order to subdue; fear thrives on attention.

Feelings are of a different source than the ego. They come from the highest and best that is within us. They are always an expression of unconditional love. Because love always overpowers fear, feelings are more powerful than emotions. When you are moved to reconcile with Aunt Tillie and treat her kindly, feeling has moved you. Spiritual qualities such as compassion, courage, openness, caring, generosity, and kindness are feelings. Self-mastery happens when you live your life from your authentic feelings, not from your reactionary emotions.

Mental

This life structure has to do with the nature of your mind. Your brain is a mechanical information processor that your mind controls. Your mind is your consciousness, the contents of your awareness. Your mind is what you use to change your life, to overcome your lower self, your fears, and your ego, and to create the best life you can. Your mind allows you to learn, to create, and to be self-correcting and self-generating. Your mind is the portal to the intuitive wisdom that will empower your life. Health in this structure means you can focus, learn, create, control your thoughts, and find peace.

Spiritual

Surveys show that most people believe in a power larger than themselves that can help with life's challenges. This structure is about your mental concept of a higher power or presence and your relationship with it. Our limited human minds cannot know that power or presence fully except through a mental concept and personal experience. But our understanding can grow, maturing into a powerful relationship that nourishes us and our vision.

Many of us operate with the God concept that we were taught as children, and that we understood with a child's mind. Unless we make a concerted effort to develop a more mature understanding that can lead to richer spiritual experiences and a better life, that's where we stay.

The experience of unity with God or a universal loving presence is the goal of the spiritual structure of life. What is your experience of a higher power? What does it provide in your life? Do you see a distinction between God and spirituality or institutionalized religion? Can you imagine a spirituality that transcends religion? If you haven't nourished the spiritual structure of life or have rejected traditional teachings, read the universe/God definition in the Introduction. It may give you a new way to approach this life structure that can benefit you and your visionbuilding journey. I want to be sure that you've considered this part of life, because I know it can be a source of the strength, comfort, and wisdom that every visionbuilders needs.

Supply

The life structure of supply is about resources for your life and especially for your vision. Supply can mean money, ideas, opportunities, experiences, and creativity. If you look at your life and notice lack or limitation, you have some work to do on the life structure of supply. There are many good reasons you may find yourself in short supply, but I'd bet they are not what you think.

Supply is not found where you might expect. It is dependent on you—not the economy, your job, your family origins, intelligence, credentials, or anything else you may tell yourself. Throughout this book, you've had many explanations and examples of how your mindset creates your experiences. Your mindset creates your experience of supply. By reconfiguring your beliefs about supply, you can experience this life structure.

If you really thought about it, wouldn't you say that your relationship with money is more about peace of mind, security, and confidence than about a specific number of dollars? Poverty consciousness exists in the very wealthy, and prosperity consciousness exits in the dirt poor. The other resources that add up to the structure of supply follow suit. Once you focus your energy and change your thinking, money flows to you, opportunities show up, resources for all your projects are there, and life gets richer in all ways. See Chapter 4: A Blank Check to Fund Your Vision. If this life structure is holding you back from your vision, please download my e-book *Cash and Consciousness: 21 Days to Abundance*. It's a 21-day program for changing your thoughts, words, and deeds that create the prosperous life that is your natural right.

Relationships

The life structure of relationships is an unavoidable opportunity for growth. Unless you are a hermit living in the wilderness, you have to be in relationships with your fellow humans in order to live. All relationships are partnerships, each party requesting, giving, or receiving. Healthy partnerships mean that each party both gives and receives, each can be authentically themselves, and each experiences harmony, caring, cooperation, peace, and fulfillment. Asking yourself how you experience partnerships will show you your blind spots in this life structure.

Do you have healthy work relationships? Do you have close friends with whom you can be authentically yourself? How do you interact with service people? Do you have an intimate partnership—a significant other or mate? What are family gatherings like for you? In my audio seminar "Sandpaper to Silk: Perfect Partnerships All the Time", I teach you a simple system for mastering the life structure of relationships by creating them from a vision. I show you how to control your mind's tendency to set up expectations for how others should act and then reacting emotionally when they don't. I show you how to create a vision statement for every significant partnership in your life and how to make that vision a reality.

Creativity

The life structure of creativity includes work, career, sports, hobbies, art, human interactions, and creative expression in any form. Brain scan studies have found that the brain of a 25-year-old and a 75-year-old are virtually identical. Aging does not cause brain function deterioration. Lack of use does.

You are innately programmed to be a creator, a problem solver, an innovator, a learner, an information processor, and a thinker. The law of physics called entropy dictates that any system (in this case your brain) will self-destruct unless new energy is added. You add new energy by exercising creativity. If nothing is being created, there is no requirement for resources, so none are offered! If you are not attracting the resources you want in your life, look at the life structure of creativity. You have a creative genius within you and a world waiting for what only you, with your unique creativity, can create.

It's easy to get on our daily mental treadmill, pounding familiar ground, uninspired. It's easy to operate on the "squeaky wheel" system too, focusing on what causes distress in the moment. It takes conscious effort to live a day of clear intention. It takes effort to say to yourself, "Today I'm focusing on my mental development. I will learn something new today," or "Today I'm focusing on my emotional well-being. I will catch myself when I feel anger and shift to peace."

Here's why it's worth the effort. It teaches who you are—a personal development powerhouse! You experience your own power as life gets better, incrementally, day-by-day, through your own intention and focus. Small changes trick your brain into accepting change more easily. The smaller the change is, the less your brain resists it, upping your chances for success. Pretty amazing, don't you think?

Life Structures: Exercise 1

Pick one area of life and set one specific betterment intention for each day—think of it as a daily vision. Write it down, right now while you're inspired. Make it a short affirmation, like the affirmation examples later in this chapter, so it will be easy to recall. Before you start each day and at least three times throughout the day, read your day's vision. Then do the stillness practice in Chapter 6, or just sit quietly for a few minutes. That's it. Let your inner guidance do the rest. Congratulate yourself at each day's end; you've done yourself and your vision some good.

Daily Vision/Betterment Intentions

Monday _____

Tuesday _____

Wednesday _____

Thursday _____

Friday _____

Saturday _____

Sunday _____

Life Structures: Exercise 2

Ask yourself "In which of the seven areas of life do I most want more power?" Approach it from the negative if you must: "Which area of life causes me the most frustration, fear, failure?" "Where do I feel most powerless?" Turn the answer around into a statement of your ideal. What would you desire most as an ideal in that aspect of your life? Write a vision statement for your selection. A vision statement is a description of what you would like to experience if life were perfect. See Chapter 9 for help.

Life Structures: Exercise 3

Step One

There is always one life structure that is calling to you more than the others. You will recognize it intuitively. Ask yourself these questions: "If my life got better in this one particular life structure, would I be happier and more fulfilled in all areas?" "Does this life structure contain most of my challenges right now?" "Do I have a thought or behavior pattern in this area that I would like to change?" "Do I feel personally empowered in this area? (The area where you feel least powerful will probably be the area you choose.)

Step Two

Create your ideal experience for this area of your life. Use descriptions of the experience rather than conditions, for example: "In my financial life I always feel powerful, never afraid. I always have more than I need. I am a good steward of money. I am free to do whatever I choose because I always have the required resources. Money comes to me doing what I love" or, in the area of relationships: "All my relationships are harmonious. I give and receive love. I accept others as they are. I have perfect intimate partnerships, all the friends I desire, and good work relationships." You get the idea. You are creating what you want, based on what you no longer want, and on your desires. Remember, it's all inner work. It is never about changing external circumstances, and it is absolutely never about changing other people.

Step Three

Work your statement into an affirmation—a positive statement in the present tense—one short clear sentence describing what you are willing to be true now: "I always experience joy at work, no matter what." "My mate and I live in complete harmony." "All my labors lead to greater prosperity." Make your affirmations into visualizations, imagined scenes of you experiencing your vision. See Chapter 6 for help.

Step Four

Create an action plan; commit one week to one action that supports your affirmation. Keep your action commitment in front of you so you won't forget to do it. In our mastermind groups, you must report back next week to the group on your action commitment. Accountability is powerful. Find a supportive partner to share your weekly commitment with, and ask your partner to help you be accountable to yourself.

More Tools

Boldness

Once I needed some "alpha male energy" to get myself back on track with a project, so I thought about the quality of boldness. I used to think of myself as kind of wimpy, not the type to take bold action. To me, boldness is both exhilarating and scary, and I learned that it's a great power tool. Boldness is part of our human hardwiring, so it's a matter of locating your inner boldness and letting it out!

Who would you be if you were just 10% bolder? What would you create? What dreams would you make real? What would you be for or against? What new ideas would you promote? What would you ask for? Who would you talk to? What would you give to the world?

Once you agree to be bolder, the surfacing of hidden fears is virtually guaranteed. They often show up as discouragement. To be discouraged means to have run out of courage. You haven't. We all possess an infinite supply. The word *courage* is from the French *coeur*, which means *heart*. So take heart—literally. Hold your new boldness in your heart, and persevere. It is only when you give up on your dreams that they fail to manifest

Celibacy List

Most people need a really good reason to be celibate, right? Well, your vision is a good reason to practice a different kind of celibacy—refraining from anything that stalls your vision. Create a list of people, places, things, beliefs, habits—everything that is not furthering your vision. That can range from what is clearly toxic to what just distracts you and pulls your attention elsewhere.

When something on your list shows up in your life, as the saying goes, "Just say no." I know what you're thinking: "Maybe I can change a habit, but I can't just eliminate people from my life, even if they do hamper my vision. They're my family, friends, and co-workers, for heaven's sake!" I get it. But here's what you can eliminate. You can work within your mindset to eliminate your reaction to their behavior. You can stop giving them the power to affect you and your vision. This is self-mastery—a key visionbuilders' skill, covered in Chapters 5 and 6.

Active Relaxation

Everyone knows it's important to relax, but there's a difference between active and passive relaxation. That difference can provide a big boost to your visionbuilding efforts.

Active relaxation relaxes one part of your mind while stimulating another. When you engage your mind with something new and unexpected, you stimulate your creativity and motivation. Active relaxation means choosing an activity that is different from your everyday challenges. That gives the part of your mind that is routinely challenged a rest. Meanwhile, you choose an activity that challenges your mind in a different way. For me, a hike in the mountains, reading a mystery novel, or aerobic dance are active relaxation activities. They are different kinds of mental challenges than the ones in my everyday life and work.

Passive relaxation is just that—passive. It gives you rest, but rest that can deaden your mind and spirit if you're not paying attention. Passive relaxation provides little to no brain stimulation. It's "zoning out," fogging your brain instead of vitalizing it. If you've ever kicked back with a six-pack of beer, a bag of cookies, and mindless television, you understand passive relaxation. Sometimes it is exactly the therapy you need and the best thing you can do for your mental health and your vision. At those times, go for it, guilt-free. What's important is paying attention to the moment and deciding which kind of relaxation applies. If you stay aware of the difference between active and passive relaxation, you can always make a conscious choice. And conscious choices build visions.

Get Mentors

Get mentors, real or imagined, living or not. That's right. Your mind won't know the difference. Find people who are living a vision similar to yours, and connect with them as best you can. Learn to ask good questions and then ask them fearlessly. Learn to prepare for conversations and stay focused so that you get what you need and use your mentor's time well.

If you can't find anyone, or you just want to have some extra fun, conjure up an imaginary mentor. Imagine his or her answers to your questions and the invisible ways in he or she encourages and supports you. It will lift your mood and might tap into a part of your mind that has insights that your conscious mind doesn't.

Complete Incomplete Cycles

There is great power in finishing all unfinished business in all seven areas of life. It frees up your energy and sets you free from whatever in your past has held your attention captive. If you chose not to complete something, set it free. Let it go so you can move on. Set priorities based only on their service to your vision. (Remember one of the WD-40® Questions is "Does this serve my vision – yes or no?")

As for getting things done, consider your personal style. Do you have a task or a relationship orientation? Are you most likely to focus more on the task at hand or on the relationships with people that surround the task? I once observed a conversation that illustrates this difference perfectly. Mary needed some information from her former husband, whom she had not spoken to in years. She mentioned this to a friend, saying she couldn't imagine calling him; it was just too hard, too uncomfortable. "Oh for heaven's sake," said her friend, "just pick up the phone and tell him what you need; he won't bite you." Mary was relationship-oriented—concerned about the human dynamics; her friend was task-oriented—just get it done!

Know your natural style, and know when to and how to switch it when a different style will be best. We all get stuck sometimes in completing things. It may help you to make up a ritual, to get yourself past your fears and override your programmed hesitations. I find it helps me to ask myself "(How) does this further my vision?"

The answer provides me with the inspiration to keep going. The biggest key to accomplishment is focus, focus, focus.

Support Team

You need a support team for all seven life structures. For example, in your financial structure, you need a good bank, lender, accountant, advisor, attorney, bookkeeper (some of these may be you, but only if you are both skilled and thrilled). Look at yours, evaluate them, and replace any that are less than excellent. Be sure that they all support your vision and your vision requirement of extreme self-care.

Leaps of Faith

My signature line is something that came to me in a flash years ago, and I've been using it ever since: "Sometimes your only available transportation is a leap of faith." When you are expanding your life and get stuck, it may be time for a leap of faith. After you have articulated a vision for your desires, after you have concentrated on building new beliefs and thoughts, after you have prayed and/or meditated, spoken affirmations, and visualized, after you've done the body work and the energy work—when you've done it all and you're still standing in the same place—take a deep breath, muster up the trust you think you don't have, and leap! You know your heart's desire lies just beyond your comfort zone. Sometimes it can feel like leaping into the abyss. Sometimes it can feel like the inner and outer resources just aren't there, and you're leaping into a terrifying chasm. Do it anyway.

Close Your Mouth and Open Your Heart

This practice has saved business relationships, friendships and marriages. It's a simple visualization that moves you from opposition to unity. It diffuses anger and moves you to a better, more neutral state of mind from which to act.

When you're angry with someone, you are focused on your differences. What divides you is all that you can see, and it makes you mad. You forget all the things that unite you, your shared humanity and shared goals. By forcing yourself to see the bigger picture, the whole of the relationship, your differences are in a larger context. Now you can make more intelligent choices about how to act.

Visualize yourself standing opposite your so-called opponent. You might even be able to feel the negative energy circulating between the two of you. I sometimes have students do this as a physical exercise with a partner. If you stand across from a partner, each of you can put your hands out, with palms against your partners palms, and push hard; you'll really get the visceral feeling of opposition.

The next step in the visualization is to imagine moving next to the person, shoulder to shoulder, looking in the same direction. Now you are looking out at the world from the same standpoint (a literal "stand point," get it?). From this vantage, you will realize your commonalities. You'll find that you share the goal of the highest outcome for the matter at hand. The energy of the relationship shifts, and you are in a better emotional state from which to choose your next thoughts and actions.

Mastermind Teams

The power of mastermind teams is undisputed. The whole is greater than the sum of its parts. The whole of a team dedicated to the vision of each member is greater than the sum of its parts. Universal power is brought to bear on your vision, and your own accountability to your vision is strengthened.

The Magic of Mastermind Teams

The mastermind concept is an ancient, proven path to success. The mastermind process is the coming together of a team of minds and hearts dedicated to an ideal, and to the support of each other. Some years ago, I read the classic book *Think and Grow Rich,* by Napoleon Hill, in which he coined the term *mastermind*. Hill studied hugely successful business leaders and found the common denominator of a carefully chosen team of other successful people dedicated to each other's good— meeting regularly to support each other. My fellow New Thought minister, the late Rev. Jack Boland, created a mastermind journal and process that were more spiritually oriented than what Hill described. Building on what I appreciated most from both works, I created a mastermind process for visionbuilders. It has evolved over the years, and you now have the opportunity to benefit from the perfected process developed from our Visionbuilders Mastermind Teams™. Of course, the process continues to evolve and refine itself, especially with groups who have been together for several years and whose members have grown significantly in their own consciousness.

Group synergy is more powerful than that of individuals working alone. Revelations, clarity, inspiration, insights, guidance, and direction are powerfully revealed through group consciousness. Through mastermind teams, individuals grow and evolve in ways that are not possible individually. Science is now documenting evidence of the phenomenon of group consciousness and collective intention. (The periodical *What Is Enlightenment?* covers this beautifully in the May–July 2004 quarterly issue.) The mastermind process uses the power of group consciousness to advance individual and collective high ideals.

The facilitated Vsionbuilders' Mastermind Team™ meeting format includes these six steps:

1.   Brief stillness meditation
2.   Presentation of a different principle each meeting and discussion of how to apply it to your goals
3.   Updates and discussion of individual vision goals, progress, roadblocks and opportunities

4. Counseling and coaching, by facilitator and then by group
5. Creation of affirmations, action steps, and self-observations and agreement to hold each other's intentions in consciousness between meetings
6. Closing meditation, by facilitator

In this model, teams focus their collective energy on each other's visions. If we are working with a board of directors or corporate group, the team is focused on the shared vision. Teams are limited in size to seven members. When there is an opening, new members are recommended by a current member or by the facilitator. If the team agrees, the potential member attends one meeting, after which all members must agree to invite the candidate to join. Membership criteria are about willingness, rather than perfection, and include being willing to do the inner and outer work to create your vision, being willing to show up (or call in, for phone teams) regularly, being willing to see and believe the highest possibilities for your team members, especially in those times when they are stuck, and being willing to accept and love your team members, no matter what.

Teams agree to abide by the following **Visionbuilders' Mastermind Team™** rules of the road:

1. Commit to attendance, preparation, daily practice, and commit to your own vision.
2. Be present for your team. Listen with an open mind and heart.
3. Practice unconditional acceptance. Transform criticism, judgment, or annoyance the instant you sense it. Think beyond personalities—both others and your own.
4. Feedback = reflection only, for example, "What I notice is . . ." or clarification or expansion questions. No criticism or commentary on what is shared—ever.
5. All requests for support are honored unconditionally. Your definition of the life you desire is your right, and it

is protected. No one on your team is permitted to judge your desires or requests.

6. Practice the attitude of seeing only the highest and best in your teammates. This supports them and activates the cosmic law of correspondence in your favor. Only the highest and best in you will be seen by your teammates

7. Confidentiality—zero tolerance. We must all know with certainty that we are safe to be ourselves, we will not be judged, and none of the meeting is shared outside.

8. Stay in touch. If you have to miss a meeting, your update, requests, and commitments—received via e-mail—will be acted on by your team.

Professional Facilitation:

I believe these teams work best with professional facilitation, with a trained visionbuilders' mastermind facilitator who does the following:

1. Manages the flow of the agenda and keeps the process on track.

2. Is not part of the team, so that he or she has no personal stake, and is able to be focused on the process.

3. Is skilled in coaching and counseling from the philosophy of the visionbuilders' program.

4. Ensures the integrity of the rules and the process, by objectively observing and guiding the meeting.

The Visionbuilders' Institute trains facilitators in our methodology and licenses the process for nominal fees. To learn more or find a licensed facilitator near you contact us at revshep@usa.net or www.visionbuildersinstitute.com.

Chapter 12

SELF-TESTS TO JUMPSTART YOUR SUCCESS

This set of self-tests provides quick and easy status indicators. They are self-awareness tools. Use them for a baseline understanding of your current beliefs and to estimate your visionbuilding progress. The tests would not hold up to scientific scrutiny, so please don't think you're taking precise, bias-free measurements. Because they are self-reported, even if you are scrupulously honest, your mindset influences your answers. Consider these tests to be proven tools for good estimates of what is true for and about you in the moment.

The Visionbuilders' You Are Here Exercise

Aren't mall directories a great invention? What's your first thought when you're in an unfamiliar shopping mall looking for a particular business? "Where's the mall directory?" They're usually large color-coded business listings, linked to a map to help you find your target. There is also an X marker that says, "You are here." That marker is the key to the whole process, because only when you know where you are can you find your target. Then you can beeline it, not wasting time or steps along the way. This visionbuilders' exercise gives you an X marker starting point for building your vision. You'll create a baseline to help you measure progress toward your vision.

The visionbuilders' You Are Here exercise works great when you have specific clear goals or a vision. But if you're a new visionbuilder, you may not have clear goals yet. You probably have some general goals, or at least a desire for a better life, so use them for now as you work through the questions. You can come back to them again and again as you build your vision. They will help you assess the strength of the foundation that you're developing as you become a more powerful visionbuilder.

The process of visionbuilding creates both inner growth and outer growth. You're growing in personal character qualities, such as wisdom and courage, and in outer measurable success. This exercise addresses both, so you'll get in the mental habit of considering both as you progress.

Instructions

Looking at your life right now, ask yourself these questions. Use whatever measurement scale you like: either a scale of 1–10, 10 meaning "always" and 1 meaning "never," or a scale of "always, sometimes, or never".

1. How much do I rely on my inner guidance? _____
2. How clear are my visions or goals? _____
3. How much self-mastery do I have? _____
4. How often do I practice spiritual connection, such as prayer, meditation, contemplation, thanksgiving? _____
5. How much do I believe in my ability to live my vision? _____
6. How much focus, time and energy am I dedicating to my vision? _____
7. How much am I giving of my unique talents, abilities, and skills? _____

As you move forward in your visionbuilding, or if you are already working toward a vision or goals, ask yourself these questions.

1. How have I grown spiritually?

    Spiritual growth means expressing more spiritual qualities, such as wisdom, patience, compassion, prosperity, or unconditional love. Think about a distinction between these qualities and qualities of the ego, such as selfishness, anger and self-righteousness. Looking back to the past three months or the past year, answer the question "In what ways have I grown spiritually?" If you have had a vision or goals, ask "How has this served my vision or goals?" For example, a counseling client of mine is focusing on unconditional acceptance of his co-workers. He might look back and observe that he used to be critical of all of them every day—that's his baseline or X marker. Now, he notices he is critical of about half of them only several times a week. That's a rough measure of progress, good enough to provide useful information and surely cause for celebration.

2. How have I grown materially?

    To answer this question, we'll define material growth as what you created that is tangible and measurable. What have you brought into being? And, if you have a vision or goals, how it has served your vision or goals? My husband and I own apartments, and we have a vision of the highest possibilities for the life of those units. Over the last year, we have installed new appliances, upgraded the landscaping, and changed management companies. This is a tangible measure of how we are serving our vision. Another measurement of material growth is that we have increased rents to reflect the upgraded living space, so each apartment now generates more income.

3. To what extent am I living a joyful life?

Joy is your goal. You'll see that it's true if you think about it. Why do you want the material goodies? The perfect harmonious relationships? The vibrant good health? Because we humans are joy-seeking machines. An unmarried coaching client of mine has a vision of a husband and family. In building that vision, she now has a family focus that wasn't there before. She teaches children's Sunday school, she is in a mastermind team with a married couple with children, she has filled her home with symbols of family, and she is dating again after a long period of solitude. She is not living fully in her vision yet, but she can look at her life at this point and say, "Yes, this is progress toward my vision."

Visionbuilders' Self-Esteem Awareness Self-Test

Self-esteem is about your relationship with you, your self-approval, and self-criticism about how you live your life. Authentic self-esteem is not egocentrism, but a humble self-appreciation. This self-test will give you a general baseline of your self-esteem. It is not a scientific test, but nonetheless a useful way to understand your beliefs about you. As you read the questions, respond according to how true each statement is for you, using the following rating scale. Be honest; tell yourself the truth.

Respond to the questions with how true the phrase is for you right now1) never, (2) occasionally, (3) usually, or (4) always.

1. I accept myself unconditionally just as I am now. _____
2. I accept others unconditionally just as they are now. _____
3. My opinion of me is more important than what others think of me. _____
4. I forgive myself for my mistakes. _____
5. I think of the past only for its pleasant memories. _____
6. I like myself, regardless of what others say or do. _____
7. I do not feel guilty for my behavior or thoughts. _____

8. I welcome failure, mistakes, and being wrong as signs of my growth. _____

9. I compare myself only to my own goals, never to other's lives. _____

10. I feel worthy and valuable, even when I don't meet my goals. _____

11. I am as important as anyone else. _____

12. I act only as my inner wisdom and natural intuition guide me. _____

13. I allow others to experience the consequences of their behavior. _____

14. I ask directly for what I want. _____

15. I see problems as opportunities. _____

16. I am flexible and eager to learn in the face of any challenges. _____

17. I see all life experiences as somehow benefitting me and my goals. _____

18. I abide by my values or standards and allow others their own. _____

19. I accept full responsibility for all of my life. _____

20. I consciously control all of my behavior, including my thoughts. _____

21. I focus on my own growth and allow others their own path. _____

22. I am curious about life, eager for experiences and expansion. _____

23. I allow others to grow on their own, not to depend on me. _____

24. I treat myself well, as evidence of my self-love. _____

25. I boldly offer my gifts to the world, confident in their value. _____

Reflection:

Each statement is a positive affirmation—a description of healthy self-esteem, so ideally you want each answer to be "always" or the number 4 response. Your answers that are otherwise can become "always" by working with the questions as affirmations.

Visionbuilders' Money Mindset Self Test 1: Poverty-Prosperity Consciousness

Use this self-test from my *Cash and Consciousness: 21 Days to Abundance* to learn more about the inner world from which you experience the outer world of money. Whatever you find, take heart. Remember, the work of this program is moving you toward a life lived from prosperity consciousness. The universe always supports your prosperity, because prosperity is your natural state.

This is not a test that will give you an exact measurement. It is designed to give you a baseline sense of your prosperity consciousness and direct you to your biggest growth opportunities. Isn't it great to learn where you need to direct your efforts?

As you read the lists that define poverty consciousness and prosperity consciousness, ask yourself "Is that always, sometimes, or never me?" Write **A**, **S**, or **N** in the space after the item.

Poverty Consciousness

1. I am not clear on what I want to be, or do, or have. _____

2. I avoid responsibility for my failure or success. _____
3. I practice procrastination, or "analysis paralysis." _____
4. I don't feel deserving or worthy. _____
5. I have only limited curiosity. _____
6. I have only limited imagination or vision. _____
7. I often am hoarding, tightfisted, or a "prophet of doom." _____

8. I don't enjoy spending money on myself. _____

9.   I feel guilty when I have money, and I also when I don't.
     _____

10. I have difficulty in receiving. _____

11. I lack excitement or enthusiasm for life. _____

12. I work at jobs I don't like just for the money. _____

Prosperity Consciousness

1.   I have enthusiastic clarity, a vision, single-minded focus.
     _____

2.   I take full responsibility for everything that happens to me. _____

3.   I take focused, timely, energetic movement toward my desires. _____

4.   I have solid self-esteem; I believe in my own value.
     _____

5.   I have boundless interest in life. _____

6.   I have expansive, creative ideas, a great imagination.
     _____

7.   I operate from the awareness of unlimited supply.
     _____

8.   My self-respect makes it comfortable to spend money on myself. _____

9.   Guilt is simply not an applicable emotion—not on my radar! _____

10. High self-worth makes it easy for me to receive.
     _____

11. I am an active, enthusiastic participant and lover of life.
     _____

12. I apply myself to work that is joyful and uses my talents fully. _____

Reflection:

Then focus on your "always" and "sometimes" answers in the Poverty Consciousness section. You have work to do there. And please, promise me you won't spend even one minute analyzing why you hold those beliefs. That will only strengthen them, because you feed them with your thought energy. Instead, work to plant healthier money beliefs in your subconscious. Find your "always" and "sometimes" poverty beliefs' opposites in the prosperity consciousness list, and get to work using them as affirmations. Speak them to yourself frequently, write them, do whatever you can to make them feel real to you. Use this technique with the rest of the program, and you'll soon be living in the abundance that you desire and deserve.

Visionbuilders' Money Mindset Self Test 2: Money Beliefs Exercise

Prosperity is the natural order of the universe, your birthright, essential to expressing your true self fully and giving your gifts to the world. If you have strayed from your natural prosperity, it is because you have accepted some false beliefs and let yourself be controlled by them. Your ego has hooked you into living in darkness instead of light. Seeing what those beliefs might be is the first step to replacing them with healthier ones. The first statements are about your money beliefs right now. Use your intuition to reveal the truth to your conscious mind. Notice there is no scale or rating system. This is not a mental exercise, but an intuitive one. Notice how each statement feels to you. Does it seem true about you? Use your gut instincts. Most of us have absorbed these beliefs from our culture, and even a small belief in any of them means that they are in your subconscious mind, where they are probably causing trouble. Getting free of them will help create prosperity.

Money Beliefs

Notice how you react to these statements. Which ones seem true for you? Ask yourself, "Do I believe this? Is it true in my experience, or only in my mind?"

- Money is the root of all evil.
- To be holy, I have to be poor.
- The "pie" is limited. If I have more than others do, they will have less.
- To have money, I must work very hard and sacrifice much.
- Wanting money is wrong. I should be humble and not want rewards for my efforts.
- Truly intelligent, talented, and spiritual people are "above" money.
- People who have a lot of money usually got it deceitfully, maybe illegally, but for sure at the expense of the poor.
- If I have a lot of money, I shouldn't act like I do; I shouldn't spend it flamboyantly or too freely.
- It is important to save for a rainy day, to sock money away because "you never know."
- "A penny saved is a penny earned."
- "A fool and his money are soon parted."
- It's OK to spend money on my dependents, family, or friends, but selfish to spend it on myself.
- If I had a lot of money, I would never have time to enjoy it; it would be a big responsibility and a hassle to manage.
- Add more such statements that occur to you.

Reflection

Reflect on your answers and what it was like to do the exercise. Observe your energy and your emotions. Which ones are the most powerful for you? Past and present, notice where your energy goes. For those you no longer believe, why not? How has life changed since you changed this belief? For those you still believe, what would be their opposite? What could you believe instead? What spiritual principles relate to the new or old belief? How could your life be different if you believed the opposite? Are you willing? Why, or why not?

Important Note

It's important to accept your existing beliefs without criticism. Lack of acceptance is condemnation, which gives power to what you don't want. Remember not to nourish beliefs that you want to extinguish. If you are holding the belief "I am terrible with money" and you get angry with yourself for that belief or struggle against it—you make it stronger! You have just affirmed the idea "I am terrible with money." Instead, when you hold all your beliefs in unconditional acceptance, not judging or struggling, you are free to prosper.

Visionbuilders' Self-Observation Worksheet

You can't change what you can't see. Yet success requires changing your "way of being" and transforming your mental, emotional, and even physical self so that it lines up with your vision. In order to think and act differently, you must be able to see how you are right now. You need a baseline. You need visibility over your current way of being so that you can make new choices that support your vision better. The self-observation worksheet helps you understand your present way of being so that you can adjust it. You can choose different thoughts and actions that support—instead of sabotage—your vision.

The self observation list will get you started; you can customize it as you progress. Work easy. Circle items that you observe about your current way of being and make a few notes. Ask yourself "What do I notice about these, as I work with my vision and in general?"

Self-Observation Checklist (Part 1)

- Feelings/emotional state/mood
- Intention strength
- Ego awareness
- Physical well-being
- Body signals

- Productivity
- Mental sharpness
- Insights
- Clarity
- Physical stamina/fatigue
- Desire to be with people
- Desire to be alone
- Desire to be active
- Desire to be still
- Awareness of God/universe
- Fears—in disguise as (???)
- Self-criticism/judgment
- Criticism/judgment of others
- Feelings of victimhood
- Confidence
- Awareness of my human personality
- Desire to analyze—need to know why
- Keeping commitments
- Finding excuses not to keep commitments
- Different relationship with food, alcohol, or other substances
- Different relationships with people
- More/less anger
- More/less love
- Feelings of joy vs. surface happiness
- What else (???)

Self-Observation Worksheet (Part Two)

These are specific follow-up questions from the preceding list:

1. What did I notice about myself in my visionbuilding efforts this week?
2. How did this affect my progress?
3. What insights does this provide for my visionbuilding efforts?
4. What visionbuilders' skills or mindset does this lead me to strengthen?

Final Thoughts

This final paragraph is one of simple encouragement. I can't offer you my dramatic personal rags-to-riches or despair-to-success story, because I don't have one. In my seminars I sometimes say I've grown by leaps and bounds—from solidly middle-class to solidly middle-class. Sometimes that gets a laugh, but I'm happy there. My growth has been in my peace of mind and in the confidence that I can create any vision that inspires me and might be of use to you. Success gurus often encourage us to think big and want more of what money can buy. I encourage you to discover a vision for your business, personal life, or whatever inspires you most today. Define your own success. Then trust that the visionbuilders' process will restore your natural state of easy, graceful accomplishment. Keep building vision after vision until you are living in joy and giving your unique gifts to your world. We need your success. Thank you.

We need your success. Thank you.

Bibliography:

HELPFUL RESOURCES FOR VISIONBUILDERS

Think and Grow Rich
Napoleon Hill
Fawcett Crest d 1960 (original © 1937)

The Power of Focus
Jack Canfield, Mark Victor Hansen, Les Hewitt
Health Communications, Inc. 2000

The Laws of Manifestation
David Spangler
Findhorn Publications 1976

The Success Principles
Jack Canfield with Janet Switzer
Harper Collins 2006

How To Meditate
Lawrence LeShan
Little Brown 1974

A Whole New Mind: Why Right-Brainers Will Rule the Future
Daniel H, Pink
Penguin 2006

Creative Mind and Success
Ernest Holmes
Dodd, Mead and Co. 1957 © 1919

Blink
Malcolm Gladwell
Little, Brown and Company 2005

The Wisdom of Crowds
James Surowiecki
Anchor Books/Random House 2005

The Teachings of Abraham
Esther and Jerry Hicks
Hay House 2005

For the Inward Journey: The Writings of Howard Thurman
Howard Thurman
Harcourt 1894, © 1947

The Ideal Made Real: Applied Metaphysics for Beginners
Christian D Larson
Newcastle Publishing 1995

Megatrends 2010: Seven Trends That Will Transform How You Work, Live and Invest
Patricia Aburdene
Hampton roads 2005

As A Man Thinketh
James Allen
Barnes and Noble 1992

Synchronicity: The Inner Path to Leadership
Joseph Jaworski
Barrett Koehler 1996

Spiritual Economics
Eric Butterworth
Unity Village Press 1989

Ordinary People as Monks and Mystics
Marsha Sinetar
Paulist Press 1986

There's a Spiritual Solution to Every Problem
Wayne Dyer
Harper Collins 2001

Cash and Consciousness: 21 Days to Abundance
Margaret Shepherd
Crowheart Media 2005 (buy on Visionbuildersinstitute.com)

Sandpaper to Silk: Perfect Partnerships All The Time (audio CD)
Margaret Shepherd
Crowheart Media 2004 (buy on Visionbuildersinstitute.com)

Five Visionbuilders Coffee Break Classes (audio CD)
Margaret Shepherd
Crowheart Media 2007 (buy on Visionbuildersinstitute.com)

BUY A SHARE OF THE FUTURE IN YOUR COMMUNITY

These certificates make great holiday, graduation and birthday gifts that can be personalized with the recipient's name. The cost of one S.H.A.R.E. or one square foot is $54.17. The personalized certificate is suitable for framing and will state the number of shares purchased and the amount of each share, as well as the recipient's name. The home that you participate in "building" will last for many years and will continue to grow in value.

Here is a sample SHARE certificate:

HABITAT FOR HUMANITY

THIS CERTIFIES THAT

YOUR NAME HERE

HAS INVESTED IN A HOME FOR A DESERVING FAMILY

1985-2005

TWENTY YEARS OF BUILDING FUTURES IN OUR
COMMUNITY ONE HOME AT A TIME

1200 SQUARE FOOT HOUSE @ $65,000 = $54.17 PER SQUARE FOOT
This certificate represents a tax deductible donation. It has no cash value.

YES, I WOULD LIKE TO HELP!

I support the work that Habitat for Humanity does and I want to be part of the excitement! As a donor, I will receive periodic updates on your construction activities but, more importantly, I know my gift will help a family in our community realize the dream of homeownership. **I would like to SHARE in your efforts against substandard housing in my community!** *(Please print below)*

PLEASE SEND ME _____ SHARES at $54.17 EACH = $ $_____

In Honor Of: _____

Occasion: (Circle One)   HOLIDAY   BIRTHDAY   ANNIVERSARY

   OTHER: _____

Address of Recipient: _____

Gift From: _____ *Donor Address:* _____

Donor Email: _____

I AM ENCLOSING A CHECK FOR $ $_____ PAYABLE TO HABITAT FOR HUMANITY <u>OR</u> PLEASE CHARGE MY VISA OR MASTERCARD *(CIRCLE ONE)*

Card Number _____ Expiration Date: _____

Name as it appears on Credit Card _____ Charge Amount $ _____

Signature _____

Billing Address _____

Telephone # Day _____ Eve _____

PLEASE NOTE: Your contribution is tax-deductible to the fullest extent allowed by law.
Habitat for Humanity • P.O. Box 1443 • Newport News, VA 23601 • 757-596-5553
www.HelpHabitatforHumanity.org

Printed in the USA
CPSIA information can be obtained
at www.ICGtesting.com
JSHW082204140824
68134JS00014B/421